WORSHIP IN THE STORM

JAY STRACK

AND

DIANE RASO STRACK

NELSON IMPACT
A Division of Thomas Nelson Publishers
Since 1798

www.thomasnelson.com

Published by Nelson Impact, a Division of Thomas Nelson, Inc., P.O. Box 141000, Nashville, TN 37214.

Unless otherwise noted, all Scripture quotations are taken from *The New King James Version.*® Copyright © 1982 by Thomas Nelson, Inc. Used by permission. All rights reserved.

Scripture quotations marked NCV are taken from *The New Century Version*®. Copyright © 2005 by Thomas Nelson, Inc. Used by permission. All rights reserved.

ISBN: 1-4185-0597-8

Printed in the United States of America

06 07 08 09 RRD 9 8 7 6 5 4 3 2 1

Page design by Crosslin Creative
2743 Douglas Lane, Thompsons Station, Tennessee 37179

CONTENTS

This study guide is dedicated
to the memory of Jeanie Allen,
who inspired all those she encountered
with hope and the love of Christ.
Jeanie left a legacy of
sharing Christ through testimony
and compassion and showed many
how to worship in the storm.
In this study, her family shares
personal insights into their own struggles
so that students might know
the peace and strength of Christ
as they navigate the very
real adversities of life.

INTRODUCTION

Sometimes life holds more questions than answers. Or, at least it seems that way. Even though trials and storms come and go in our lives and we find ourselves looking for answers to hard questions, God longs to give us

peace,

confidence,

wisdom,

and joy in the journey.

If you're going through something hard right now, fear and worry might be the dominant emotions of your heart. We totally understand! But in this hard time, God wants to show you something so much greater than you can imagine. In this study guide, you will learn that God's promises are true and He truly cares for you. And this knowledge and understanding of who God is will completely and powerfully transform your life.

Adversity will no longer be seen as an obstacle; instead, you will recognize adversity as an opportunity to watch the power of God in action. Through every emotional and spiritual situation you may face, learn to believe that the bigger your God is, the smaller your obstacles are. Let the journey begin!

KEY

STUDENT LEADERSHIP UNIVERSITY CURRICULUM

Throughout this study guide, you will see several icons or headings that represent an idea, a statement, or a question that we want you to consider as you experience Scripture in this study guide series. Refer to the descriptions below to help you remember what the icons and headings mean.

transfuse (trans FYOOZ) : to cause to pass from one to another; transmit

The goal of the lesson for the week.

Experience Scripture: Learning to really experience Scripture is the key element to "getting" who God is and all that He has in store for you.

infuse (in FYOOZ) : to cause to be permeated with something (as a principle or quality) that alters usually for the better

Through journaling, group discussion, and personal study, experience Scripture as it permeates your heart and alters your life.

Future Tense Living: Your choices today will determine your future. Learn how to live with dynamic purpose and influence.

Attitude Reloaded: Rethink your attitude! Learn to replace self-centered, negative, or limited thoughts with positive, courageous, compassionate thoughts that are based on God's unlimited ability and power.

 In His Steps: Every attitude and action of your life should begin with the questions, How would Jesus respond to this person and situation before me? What would He choose to do?

diffuse (di FYOOZ): to pour out and permit or cause to spread freely; to extend, scatter

Once God's Word is infused into your heart, it will pour forth to others without restraint. In this section, explore what that looks like in your daily life.

 Called to Lead: Learn how to lead others as Christ would.

 Called to Stand: Know what you believe and learn how to defend it with clarity and strength.

Called to Share: Sharing truth and serving others are results of a transformed life. How can you share with others the awesome things you're learning?

One Thing: Consider ONE THING you can do this week to make a difference in your life and/or the life of another.

[FUSE BOX]

Power up for the week with this focused truth.

CHAPTER 1

STUFF HAPPENS

WHY DO BAD THINGS HAPPEN TO GOOD PEOPLE?

KEY SCRIPTURE

"For My thoughts are not your thoughts, nor are your ways My ways," says the Lord. "For as the heavens are higher than the earth, so are My ways higher than your ways, and My thoughts than your thoughts."
—Isaiah 55:8–9

IT COULD BE YOU!

As a young boy who experienced six broken homes (yes, I know it sounds like a soap opera, but that's only because it was!), I spent much of my childhood and teen years on the decks of commercial fishing boats that belonged to various stepdads, some of whom I don't even remember now. Probably, I just choose not to remember them any longer.

On the deck of a ship in the middle of an ocean or gulf somewhere, I spent many evenings staring at the stars and trying to figure out the many questions of life.

✦ *Why am I here?*

✦ *What does the future hold?*

✦ *Why did this God they say is so powerful allow my life to get so out of control?*

I never doubted there was a Creator or that He was powerful. Living on the sea, studying the heavens, and watching the incredible beauty and variety of creation told me He was real.

But I did doubt that I mattered to Him.

Each night on the fishing boats, there was a sorting process. Some fish made it, and some didn't. Those that didn't were thrown overboard because they didn't sell well—too many bones, too difficult to clean, or too strong a flavor. As I watched the sorting process, I was painfully aware that I might be once again sorted from my family just like those fish—too much trouble, not well liked.

> All the inhabitants of the earth are reputed as nothing; He does according to His will in the army of heaven and among the inhabitants of the earth. No one can restrain His hand or say to Him, "What have You done?"
>
> —Daniel 4:35

Some days and nights the storms we faced on the boats were so severe that I thought we wouldn't live through them. I couldn't wait to get to land. But then I found out that life on shore held storms of its own.

The broken homes I lived in led to many fights, moving from one town to another, abandonment, and abuse. I was physically abused, sexually abused by a temporary stepbrother, labeled as slow, and the victim of much verbal abuse. Trust me, the storms in my life were just as real as the storms I encountered on the ocean. I don't know which was harder to live through.

The hardest part was trying to understand why this stuff was happening to me. I was just a kid. Didn't anyone really care?

WHY KNOW IT?

Adversity is defined as:

✦ A state or condition contrary to one of well-being.[1]

✦ A state of hardship or affliction; misfortune. A calamitous event.[2]

transfuse (trans FYOOZ): to cause to pass from one
to another; transmit

On the bridge from childhood to adulthood, we become painfully aware that life can be disappointing and challenging. Because you have never experienced these adversities before, even a small conflict or problem can throw you off track emotionally.

Some of the adversities you might face as a teenager are:

✦ Death of a family member or friend

✦ Divorce

✦ Injury

✦ Personal or family illness

✦ Decrease in family income

✦ Friendship/relationship issues

✦ Learning differences

✦ Financial stress

✦ Feelings of depression or hopelessness

✦ Family conflict

✦ Disappointment in people

> As you do not know what is the way of the wind, or how the bones grow in the womb of her who is with child, so you do not know the works of God who makes everything.
> —Ecclesiastes 11:5

In a matter of moments, you go from innocent childhood to the thought that life can't get any worse. That's when frustration takes over and doubt pours in. You think, *How can a kind and just God allow me to be in this situation?*

Don't feel embarrassed or guilty about this natural response. Even Jesus uttered on the cross, "My God, My God, Why have You forsaken Me?" (Matthew 27:46).

"For My thoughts are not your thoughts, nor are your ways My ways," says the Lord. "For as the heavens are higher than the earth, so are My ways higher than your ways, and My thoughts than your thoughts." —Isaiah 55:8–9

God is God. We will not understand all of His workings in this life, but all will be revealed to us in eternity. So what do we do in the meantime? Don't fret! He has given us all that we need to not only navigate the storms in life, but to worship Him as we go through them as well.

infuse (in FYOOZ): to cause to be permeated with something (as a principle or quality) that alters usually for the better

Three "Why" Questions
There are three *why* questions that tend to take over our thought patterns when we are faced with difficult circumstances:

1. Why did God let this happen?

2. Why doesn't God care?

3. Why is there evil in the world?

1. Why did God let this happen?
The first question of *why* may never be answered in this life. We can ask it over and over and torture ourselves with the need for an answer, but the reality is that we simply might not get one.

God tells us, "I am God. Trust Me." Our faith multiplies when we understand the majesty of God and the fullness of His power.

If you don't get your question of why answered, how will it affect you? Are you willing to believe that God wants the best for you and that He will work good for you even in difficult times?

THINK ABOUT IT

God has demonstrated His great power through creation. You see it everywhere:

- ✦ Animals so different and unique;

- ✦ The grand beauty of nature;

- ✦ Science that reveals the intricate workings of His creation;

- ✦ The human body so complex that it has the ability to heal itself and to reproduce;

- ✦ Stars that hang in place next to planets in a sky so vast it has no end;

- ✦ Immense oceans with powerful currents and multitudes of living beings, all wonderfully different.

List at least three things in nature or science that help you to understand how powerful and creative God is. Describe why they are fascinating to you or unique. What makes that part of God's creation speak to you about His power?

1 _____

2 _____

3 _____

When the world seems difficult and evil, then take some time aside to do nothing but let the wonder of creation take over your mind.

Choose ONE THING for which you can be thankful for—your family, friends, health, God's mercy, His love, His judgment, His patience, etc.—and focus on it throughout the week.

2. Why doesn't God care?

The second *why* question has already been answered. We never need ask it again, for God proved His love for us by sending His Son, Jesus, who willingly endured the pain of the cross.

Does God care about you? *Absolutely!*

The real question is, do we have the right to cross-examine this God who has already revealed His great love for us, who has sent His Son to die in our place?

The Bible says that Jesus was "wounded for our transgressions" (Isaiah 53:5) and "suffered once for sins, the just for the unjust, that He might bring us to God" (1 Peter 3:18). The word *suffering* comes from the Latin word that means to bear up under work or illness. It was also used to describe a penalty or an expense in the form of a punishment.

Christ has indeed suffered for us. When we understand the scope of His love, then we get to *know* Him personally and understand the power of it.

3. Why is there evil in the world?

In the Bible, God is described as loving, good, and compassionate.

✦ "But God demonstrates His own love toward us, in that while we were still sinners, Christ died for us" (Romans 5:8).

✦ "The kindness and the love of God our Savior toward man appeared" (Titus 3:4).

✦ "Behold what manner of love the Father has bestowed on us, that we should be called children of God!" (1 John 3:1).

✦ "He who does not love does not know God, for God is love" (1 John 4:8).

OK, we believe God is love. But why is there so much hate in the world, why so much evil?

When circumstances cause a crisis, and a crisis leads to a whirlwind of confusion, Satan is quick to rush in and whisper accusations against God's love for you. His favorite strategy is to make us feel victimized by God and even abandoned by Him. Don't fall into his trap, but instead, understand and stand on the simple answer found in God's Word.

> *The heavens declare the glory of God; and the firmament shows His handiwork.*
> —Psalm 19:1

The Bible begins with the assuring words, "In the beginning, God created the heavens and the earth" (Genesis 1:1). Over and over in the early chapters, we read, "It was good." God indeed created a perfect world.

Well, it was perfect, except for one thing—man was in it. Adam and Eve, created with a free will, lived in paradise. We don't know how long it took before they listened to Satan's whispers and rejected the Word of God, the way of God and the will of God, but they did.

God did not create evil, but He did allow free choice and the potential for evil.[3] Man has the right every day to choose to love or hate, to do good or evil.

diffuse (di FYOOZ); to pour out and permit or cause to spread freely; to extend, scatter

The contrast of God's love with the overwhelming evil in the world causes us to over and over ask *why?* Dr. James Dobson calls this "the betrayal barrier," the sense that God is abandoning us in the midst of the storms of life. Nothing could be further from the truth.

The apostle Paul, who endured imprisonment, illness, beatings, and all manner of evil, gives his best advice for answering the *whys* of life in Hebrews 12:3: "Consider Him (Jesus) who endured such hostility from sinners against Himself, lest you become weary and discouraged in your souls."

> Worship is setting your mind's attention and your heart's affection on the Lord, praising Him for Who He is and what He has done.
> —Louie Giglio

Paul tells us to "consider" Christ—that is, to reckon up, to count up, to compare, to weigh. The word appears only once in the New Testament and no doubt it was chosen carefully.[4]

Worship in the Storm

God wants us to seriously meditate on the love of Christ, on His suffering for us, His death on the cross, His resurrection, and His personal, intimate call to us in salvation and to *compare or weigh* this out against the temporary setbacks and pain we are facing.

✦ *Consider* all that He has done for the world.

✦ *Consider* all that He has already done for you personally.

During a hurricane devastation recovery interview, Author Rick Warren (*Purpose-Driven Life*) was asked by Larry King, CNN host, "What do you say to these hurting people?" Rick said, "Count up what's left, not what's lost, and focus on that. Put your hope in what cannot be taken away, your personal faith in Christ."

Simple, clear advice. That's what Paul was trying to say when he said *consider Jesus* in these difficult days, or you will find yourself *weary and discouraged,* ready to quit and give up on life.

FUSE BOX

Your journey to peace in the *whys* of life begins today as you spend time this week *considering* or *counting up* all that Christ has already done for you.

PRIVATE WORLD DEVOTIONS

MONDAY: See it. Read the surrounding passages or chapter for the Key Scripture so that you can get an understanding of the background and context. This helps you to really *see* the verse.

TUESDAY: Hear it. Read the daily Key Scripture and/or surrounding passage out loud, putting your name in, if applicable. For example, <u>John</u> *can do all things through Christ. Thieves have come to destroy* <u>John</u>, *but Jesus has come that* <u>John</u> *might have eternal life.*

WEDNESDAY: Write it. Write the verse and then what it says about:

- ✦ *Others:* Respond, serve, and love as Jesus would.
- ✦ *Me:* Specific attitudes, choices, or habits.
- ✦ *God:* His love, mercy, holiness, peace, joy, etc.

PRIVATE WORLD JOURNAL

*I am grateful for—I praise You for—I am
feeling—I am thinking—I need help with*

PRIVATE WORLD DEVOTIONS *(Continued)*

THURSDAY: Memorize it. Take the verse with you—write it on a card or put it in your phone, iPod, or PDA. Go over it throughout the day so that it begins to *live* in your heart and mind.

FRIDAY: Pray it. Personalize the verse as you pray for yourself or for others or in praise to God. To pray is literally "to think about." Try thinking out loud or writing in your **PRIVATE WORLD JOURNAL.**

SATURDAY: Share it. Ask the Lord to bring someone to mind or in your path today who needs good news. Don't be shy—just let it out! Whether you IM, write, text, tell, or send it, the joy of God's Word will flow from your heart into theirs.

PRAYER REQUESTS

Date	Name	Need	Answer

PRIVATE WORLD JOURNAL

*I am grateful for—I praise You for—I am
feeling—I am thinking—I need help with*

NOTES

CHAPTER 2

STUFF HAPPENS
WHY DOES IT HAVE TO HAPPEN TO ME?

KEY SCRIPTURE

These things I have spoken to you, that in Me you may have peace. In the world you will have tribulation; but be of good cheer, I have overcome the world.
—John 16:33

IT COULD BE YOU!

"My mom was thirty-eight years old when she was first diagnosed with cancer. I was in third grade, and none of it made sense to me. I could not understand why everyone was so upset and why it was such a big deal. When my mom lost her hair . . . now, that was a little weird. My dad was so loving with Mom. He cared for her and loved her and even shaved his own head while she was without hair—they were a real pair!

"I never heard my mother ask, 'Why me?' but I am certain that she must have wondered it. I have heard my dad say that we are all in one of three stages of life, all the time. We are either going into troubles, in the middle of troubles, or just coming out of troubles.

> You ask, "Why me?"
>
> The truth is, "Why not you?"

"I'm sure that Jesus didn't come to keep my mom from having cancer or to keep me out of troubles; He came to go through them with me. My mom used to tell my dad that she was never, ever alone in all those trips to a chemotherapy room. She always told us of some other person with a greater need than hers." (As told by Amy Allen, used with permission.)

WHY KNOW IT?

✦ Depression affects approximately one in eight teens in North America.[1]

✦ The more deeply committed a person is to evangelical Christianity, the more at ease they report being with their life circumstances.[2]

transfuse (trans FYOOZ): to cause to pass from one to another; transmit

When adversity surrounds you, you might feel isolated and alone. You may be asking:

✦ Am I the only one who hurts?

✦ Doesn't anyone care or understand?

✦ Why did she make the cheerleading squad, but I didn't?

✦ Why do they have parents who love each other and stay together, but I don't?

✦ Why did I study and still fail the test, but he didn't study and passed?

✦ Why is my mom/dad/loved one sick, and theirs is healthy?

✦ Why did my friend have to die? Why is she/he the only one in the class to die so young?

✦ Why did my boyfriend/girlfriend break up with me and I'm the only one without a date?

✦ Why did my dad lose his job, and they all have plenty of money?

✦ Why does everyone else have a car, but we can't afford one?

✦ Why didn't I make the team, but everyone else who tried out did?

✦ Why can't I make good grades like my brother/friend/sister?

When you're facing difficult circumstances, just walking down the hall at school, watching students laugh and having fun, can hurt. Why are they happy and you're not? All of a sudden, canned answers, pats on the back, and quick fixes no longer work.

Life isn't fair! But whoever promised it would be?

These things I have spoken to you, that in Me you may have peace. In the world you will have tribulation; but be of good cheer, I have overcome the world. —**John 16:33**

Notice that in this verse, Jesus didn't say, "*If* you have tribulation," or "You *might* have tribulation." No, He told His disciples, "You *will* have tribulation." It's a given—everyone who lives in this world will experience tribulation, or hard times, at some point in life.

And as Christians, we have an even higher likelihood of experiencing difficulty in this world. As the apostle Paul said, "*All* who desire to live godly in Christ Jesus *will suffer persecution*" (2 Timothy 3:12; emphasis added).

"All" is a little word, but it has a big meaning—you and every other Christian! There are no exceptions: every person who follows Christ in this world will experience tribulation, suffering, and persecution at some point in life.

THINK ABOUT IT

✦ Why should you be exempt from adversity when no one else is?

_____

_____

_____

✦ Why should you be exempt from adversity when Jesus wasn't?

_____

_____

_____

infuse (in FYOOZ) : to cause to be permeated with something (as a principle or quality) that alters usually for the better

What Did I Do?

A *false view of God* causes us to feel that anytime adversity occurs, it is the result of something we did.

Really, think about this. Do you really think that the whole world revolves around you? Does it make sense that whatever you choose to do can bring about adversity in the lives of others? Do you have an image of God as an angry judge standing by ready to pour judgment on you?

The *truth about God* is that He loves you personally and intensely. He wants the best for you and longs to bless you. Jesus says, "Be of good cheer, I have overcome the world" (John 16:33).

The first thing we usually do in adversity is tell a friend our problems. Often the results are disastrous, ranging from pointed fingers to gossip to betrayal by the friend.

Just ask Job. His friends told him that all the disaster and heartache in his life must be the result of Job's sin. They told him, "Who ever perished being innocent? Or where were the upright ever cut off?" (Job 4:7). In other words, "Job, you must have done something wrong!"

Even Jesus' disciples assumed that a man's blindness was because of sin. They asked Jesus, " Rabbi, who sinned, this man or his parents, that he was born blind?" (John 9:2).

Listen carefully to what Jesus answered: "Neither this man nor his parents sinned, but that the works of God should be revealed in him" (John 9:3). In other words, believing that everything that happens is a result of God's punishment is just plain wrong.

There are two very different, in fact, opposite points of view here.

✦ Adversity is a result of man's sin. (*Possibly, but not necessarily.*)

✦ Adversity is the opportunity to see God at work. (*True, always!*)

When you look at adversity from your own point of view, then you are sure to have a pity party. These parties are almost always held alone, and the result is sure depression.

But when you look at difficulty from God's point of view, you see that adversity is not an *obstacle* in your life; it's an *opportunity* for God to work!

I Just Want to Be Like Everyone Else!

In the Bible, a woman named Hannah was so depressed that she was "in bitterness of soul" (1 Samuel 1:10). Her depression was so deep that it was poisoning her.

What could be so painful that it caused her soul to become bitter? She had no children.

> *Peninnah had children, but Hannah had no children. And her rival also provoked her severely, to make her miserable, because the Lord had closed her womb. So it was year by year when she went up to the house of the Lord that she provoked her; therefore she [Hannah] wept and did not eat. . . . And she was in bitterness of soul and prayed to the Lord and wept in anguish.* **—1 Samuel 1:2, 6–7, 10**

In Hannah's day, having a child was a big deal. In her culture, a woman's purpose was to provide children, especially male children, to her husband. Those who did not or could not were looked down upon and even thought to have sin in their lives.

Hannah never stopped to ask herself *why* she was so depressed:

Was it because she couldn't have children or because she was embarrassed?

Was it a desire for a baby or a lack of self-esteem?

Day after day Hannah listened to the snickers and snide remarks. "You can't give your husband a child. What kind of woman are you?" they would taunt. The mocking was unbearable. As a result:

✦ Hannah was a *victim* of criticism; Penninah was just plain mean.

✦ She became her own *villain*; she allowed herself to believe the gossip.

✦ She was a *volunteer*:

> ➤ She would not control her thinking patterns;

> ➤ She gave more importance to opinion than to God's Word;

> ➤ She disconnected from a healthy relationship with her husband;

> ➤ She stopped eating and became miserable.

Some people try to bully their way through life. Bullies pick on someone else as a way to get power, to get their way, or to feel important. If you're a guy, imagine your manhood being called into question because you haven't grown as fast as others or because you vow to stay morally pure.

There are girls who put down other girls even to the point of shutting them out of friendships. This rejection can be painful and difficult, particularly when you didn't do anything to deserve the criticism. This hurts and makes it hard to be happy. These are the same depressing feelings that Hannah felt.

Can you relate to Hannah's feelings of comparison and insecurity? Have you ever felt this way because of the words or opinion of others? Ask yourself, "How much of this stuff is active in me right now?" Write it:

_____

_____

_____

_____

_____

_____

Am I a **victim** of criticism?

Am I my own **villain** because I give too much importance to what they say?

Am I a **volunteer** who:

- ✦ Will not control my thinking patterns;
- ✦ Gives more importance to opinion than to God's Word;
- ✦ Disconnects from healthy relationships;
- ✦ Stops healthy habits and becomes miserable?

How am I responding to my circumstances?

Do you think you might have ever made someone else feel this way?

What did you say?

> No one can make you feel inferior without your consent.
> —Eleanor Roosevelt

What do you need to do about it?

Proverbs 23:7 says, "For as [a person] thinks in his heart, so is he." And that works for both good and bad thoughts.

Renewing the mind from unhealthy thinking is part of God's healing in our lives. The apostle Paul urges us to "not conform any longer to the patterns of this world, but be transformed by the renewing of your mind" (Romans 12:2).

I Feel So Helpless!

If these types of thoughts and labels are filling your mind like a car radio on scan, then you have to *decide* to reset the channels!

✦ God created you in His image!

✦ He has a plan for you!

What would you rather focus on:

✦ being created in the image of God?

or

✦ man's opinions?

---

diffuse (di FYOOZ) : to pour out and permit or cause to spread freely; to extend, scatter

---

It's Time for a Change!

> *Hannah answered . . . "I am a deeply troubled woman, and I was telling the Lord about all my problems." . . . Eli answered, "Go! I wish you well. May the God of Israel give you what you asked of him." Hannah said, "May I always please you." When she left and ate something, she was not sad anymore.* —**1 Samuel 1:15–18 NCV**

Wow! Hannah's change of perspective was quick! How did she go from completely bummed out to a joyful attitude? The same way you can.

Here are the **ABCs** to transforming unhealthy thinking patterns:

Always go to God with your doubt and pain. He is already listening.

Believe that pleasing God is better than pleasing man.

Change your habits, your mind, and your attitude.

Hannah did not *adapt* to the situation . . .

she was *transformed* by it . . .

and the result was incredible joy.

 You Can Do This!

When you go through adversity:

✦ Allow yourself to process the bad news. You will go through denial, anger, and depression— often more than once. This is normal and to be expected.

✦ Give yourself time to process your feelings, and don't feel rushed.

✦ Believe God has an excellent outcome for the situation.

Bad news I need to process:

When all of earth turns against you, all of heaven turns toward you.
—Max Lucado

What is ONE THING about my circumstances I cannot change this week?

_____

_____

_____

What is ONE attitude change about my circumstances that I can change this week?

_____

_____

_____

When God Intervenes, the Answer Is Abundant
Not only did God answer Hannah's prayers for a child, but He did so with abundance. In fact, He gave her **three sons and two daughters!** (1 Samuel 2:21).

Are you surprised? You shouldn't be!
  Get this:

- ✦ God loves you intensely, intimately, personally, and unconditionally.

- ✦ He is the Creator who wants to bless and care for you.

When you turn to Him by faith with a pure heart, He will bless you.

Adversity Is Not Forever

Here is Hannah's psalm of thanksgiving:

The Lord has filled my heart with joy;

I feel very strong in the Lord.

I can laugh at my enemies;

*I am glad because you have
helped me!* —**1 Samuel 2:1 NCV**

WORSHIP IN THE STORM

Decide today to worship in the midst of the storm by trusting God and giving Him thanks: Write your name in the blank below and claim this psalm as your own:

The Lord has filled _____ heart with joy;

I feel very strong in the Lord.

I can laugh at my enemies;

_____ is glad because God has helped me.[3]

Do you know someone who needs a transformed thinking pattern? Take the time to for pray for that person each day this week and get ready to share the ABCs of transforming unhealthy thinking patterns and to share your own testimony of victory.

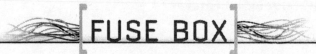

FUSE BOX

Believe that the Lord will fill you with believing the
best about Him, His plans for you, and about your
own potential and worth.

NOTES

I'm coming back
to the heart of
worship, and it's all
about You, it's all
about You, Jesus.
—Matt Redman

PRIVATE WORLD DEVOTIONS

MONDAY: See it. Read the surrounding passages or chapter for the Key Scripture so that you can get an understanding of the background and context. This helps you to really *see* the verse.

TUESDAY: Hear it. Read the daily Key Scripture and/or surrounding passage out loud, putting your name in, if applicable. For example, <u>John</u> *can do all things through Christ. Thieves have come to destroy* <u>John</u>, *but Jesus has come that* <u>John</u> *might have eternal life.*

WEDNESDAY: Write it. Write the verse and then what it says about:

✦ *Others:* Respond, serve, and love as Jesus would.

✦ *Me:* Specific attitudes, choices, or habits.

✦ *God:* His love, mercy, holiness, peace, joy, etc.

PRIVATE WORLD JOURNAL

I am grateful for—I praise You for—I am feeling—I am thinking—I need help with

PRIVATE WORLD DEVOTIONS *(Continued)*

THURSDAY: Memorize it. Take the verse with you—write it on a card or put it in your phone, iPod, or PDA. Go over it throughout the day so that it begins to *live* in your heart and mind.

FRIDAY: Pray it. Personalize the verse as you pray for yourself or for others or in praise to God. To pray is literally "to think about." Try thinking out loud or writing in your **PRIVATE WORLD JOURNAL.**

SATURDAY: Share it. Ask the Lord to bring someone to mind or in your path today who needs good news. Don't be shy—just let it out! Whether you IM, write, text, tell, or send it, the joy of God's Word will flow from your heart into theirs.

PRAYER REQUESTS

Date	Name	Need	Answer

PRIVATE WORLD JOURNAL

I am grateful for—I praise You for—I am feeling—I am thinking—I need help with

NOTES

CHAPTER 3

I KNOW THE VERSES

WHY AM I SO AFRAID?

KEY SCRIPTURE

Ah, LORD God! Behold, You have made the heavens and the earth by Your great power and outstretched arm. There is nothing too hard for You.

—Jeremiah 32:17

IT COULD BE YOU!

One week before Missy's surgery, she and her dad went to the mountains for some adventure. They knew that life would be different for a while, and that even after Missy's surgery there would be things she could no longer do. Missy tells it like this:

Tossing and turning in the hotel bed, Dad could hear me in the other room. "What's wrong, honey?" he asked.

I had to be honest and told him, "Dad, I'm afraid. Is God mad at me? Am I being punished for something I did?" Dad sat on the bed next to me and opened his Bible to Isaiah 41:10: "Fear not, for I am with you; be not dismayed, for I am your God. I will strengthen you, Yes, I will help you, I will uphold you with My righteous right hand." We talked about what it means to *fear not*, and for the first time in my life, the Word of God became very real and personal to me. I remembered my personal salvation as a child, but this was different. I needed God and He came through with His Word, filling my heart with peace.

"But Dad," I said, "what if a few days from now, I become afraid again?"

Dad laughed and said, "God has got you covered. There are 365 *fear nots* in the Bible. One for each day!" With that piece of information, I slept through the night and went into surgery a week later with peace.

WHY KNOW IT?

✦ As of mid-2005, there were eight major wars under way, with as many as two dozen "lesser" conflicts ongoing, with varying degrees of intensity.[1]

✦ More than one out of every 20 high school students—5.4 percent—skipped at least one day of school because of safety concerns in 2003.[2]

transfuse (trans FYOOZ) : to cause to pass from one to another; transmit

No doubt there are days when the world seems out of control. War, pestilence, famine, and disaster can be found anywhere and everywhere.

Let's bring that all down to you personally. Not only do you have to process the feelings of despair that the media brings to you, but you have your own personal adversity to deal with.

Sometimes you deal with small things, like:

✦ a gossiping friend

✦ an immature date

✦ appearance issues

✦ overprotective parents

✦ learning differences

Other days you face more serious situations, such as:

+ death of a close family member or friend

+ divorce or abandonment

+ injury

+ illness

+ decrease in family income

+ relationship heartbreak

When you face these difficult circumstances, it feels like you are processing conflicting or opposite facts:

+ God is loving, cares for you, and has you in His hand.

+ You face real pain, suffering, and discouragement.

Which is true? They *both* are.

As a Christian, you are looking for the "all clear" signal, but instead you keep hearing "storm warnings ahead." You can't help but ask:

+ Is God really who He says He is?

+ Is He able to do anything about my problems?

+ Is He still in control?

Don't be embarrassed if you have asked yourself these questions or felt serious doubt about God before. It is natural in the face of stress and hardship to doubt or ask questions.

This report about Him [Jesus] went throughout
all Judea and all the surrounding region.
Then the disciples of John reported to him
concerning all these things. And John [the
Baptist], calling two of his disciples to him, sent
them to Jesus, saying, "Are You the Coming
One, or do we look for another?" . . . And
that very hour He cured many of infirmities,
afflictions, and evil spirits; and to many blind
He gave sight. Jesus answered and said to
them, "Go and tell John the things you have
seen and heard: that the blind see, the lame
walk, the lepers are cleansed, the deaf hear,
the dead are raised, the poor have the gospel
preached to them. And blessed is he who is not
offended because of Me." **—Luke 7:17–23**

John the Baptist, a mighty prophet called of God to pro-
claim, or "make way" the ministry of Christ, also had
doubts. This man, John, preached and saw many come
to repentance. He lived for God, and called out those
living in sin. Jesus Himself called him a great man: "Assuredly, I say to you, among those born of women there
has not risen one greater than John the Baptist" (Matthew 11:11).

But there came a day when John the Baptist was put
in prison for that preaching, and the news was that his
head would be given as a thank-you gift for Salome after
she danced and pleased Herod.

infuse (in FY00Z)¦ to cause to be permeated with something
(as a principle or quality) that alters usually for the better

Imagine this. You live in the wilderness, sacrifice a cozy lifestyle to be a prophet of God, see God using you in mighty ways, and the next day you are imprisoned and find out that your head is to be served on a platter to satisfy a wicked woman's request. How would you feel?

In the face of this adversity, John the Baptist was experiencing doubt. Was Jesus really who He said He was? John sent word from prison through his friends to ask Jesus, "Are You the Coming One, or do we look for another?" (Luke 7:19).

Jesus didn't get angry with John. He didn't say, "Shame on you for doubting!" No, He understood and gave John this response: "Go and tell John the things you have seen and heard: that the blind see, the lame walk, the lepers are cleansed, the deaf hear, the dead are raised, the poor have the gospel preached to

> *Ah, Lord God! Behold, You have made the heavens and the earth by Your great power and outstretched arm. There is nothing too hard for You.*
> —Jeremiah 32:17

them" (Luke 7:21–22). Jesus wanted John to focus on the powerful works of God and not on the anger and evil of men.

Who is this God that we are to trust in? Is He in control, or is there no hope?

If God is not in control, then who is? Luck? Chance?

Is there a problem, challenge, or difficulty that you are facing right now that you are having trouble trusting God about?

_____

_____

_____

_____

_____

Look at Who God Is, Not What the Circumstances Are
Throughout the Bible, God is called by many names, which demonstrate who He is. Some of God's names, in the Hebrew Old Testament, include:

✦ *El Elyon*—Most High God

✦ *El Shaddai*—God Almighty

✦ *El Olam*—Everlasting God

✦ *El Roi*—The God Who Sees

✦ *El Gibbor*—God of Strength

✦ *Elohim*—The Strong One

✦ *Jehovah*—Self-existent or Eternal One

✦ *Jehovah Rapha*—The God Who Heals

Do any of these names speak of "luck?" Do you see random chance in these names? No, you see power, compassion, authority, and love.

Imagine a line down the center of your life. On one side place all the things you cannot control. List them:

_____

_____

_____

Now, list all that you **can** control:

_____

_____

_____

That's a much shorter list!

> Thus says the Lord:
> "Heaven is My
> throne, And earth is
> My footstool."
> —Isaiah 66:1

diffuse (di FYOOZ): to pour out and permit or cause to spread freely; to extend, scatter

What Should I Do When I Doubt?

1. *Choose what you will believe.* Remember, you are not the first person to doubt.

2. *Believe God is who He said He is.* If He is not, then He is a liar. Which is it?

3. *Take God at His Word.* What He says He will do, He will do.

4. *Replace doubt and weakness with faith and strength.* Feed your faith, and you starve your doubts.

> *Therefore many of His disciples, when they heard this, said, "This is a hard saying; who can understand it?" . . . From that time many of His disciples went back and walked with Him no more. Then Jesus said to the twelve, "Do you also want to go away? But Simon Peter answered Him, "Lord, to whom shall we go? You have the words of eternal life. Also we have come to believe and know that You are the Christ, the Son of the living God." —***John 6:66, 68–69***

In his response to Jesus, Peter used two very important words: *believe* and *know*:

Doubt = weakness

Faith = strength

✦ **believe**—to trust, to be faithful and true

✦ **know**—to be sure, have confidence in, to understand

Both are possible when we take God at His word!

It is ONE THING to think of the great power of God, of His mighty omnipotence, but quite another to believe that it is His good pleasure to use that power on your personal behalf.

Believe That You Are Important to God

✦ He is faithful to love you.

For I am persuaded that neither death nor life, nor angels nor principalities nor powers, nor things present nor things to come, nor height nor depth, nor any other created thing, shall be able to separate us from the love of God which is in Christ Jesus our Lord. **—Romans 8:38–39**

✦ He is faithful to care for you.

And I will pray the Father, and He will give you another Helper [the Holy Spirit], that He may abide with you forever. **—John 14:16**

✦ He is faithful to help you make it through difficulty.

No temptation has overtaken you except such as is common to man; but God is faithful, who will not allow you to be tempted beyond what you are able, but with the temptation will also make the way of escape, that you may be able to bear it. **—1 Corinthians 10:13**

WORSHIP IN THE STORM

Believe That You Can Trust God Every Day, in Every Circumstance

Rehearse the goodness of God in your life up until now, and thank Him often. This will remind you of His faithfulness in your life and His personal love for you and will promote emotional and spiritual strength.

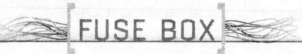

[FUSE BOX]

God has a *fear not* for you every day, in every circumstance of life.

NOTES

"Courage is not the lack of fear but the ability to face it."
—Lt. John B. Putnam Jr.
(1921–1944)

PRIVATE WORLD DEVOTIONS

MONDAY: See it. Read the surrounding passages or chapter for the Key Scripture so that you can get an understanding of the background and context. This helps you to really *see* the verse.

TUESDAY: Hear it. Read the daily Key Scripture and/or surrounding passage out loud, putting your name in, if applicable. For example, <u>John</u> *can do all things through Christ. Thieves have come to destroy* <u>John</u>, *but Jesus has come that* <u>John</u> *might have eternal life.*

WEDNESDAY: Write it. Write the verse and then what it says about:

✦ *Others:* Respond, serve, and love as Jesus would.

✦ *Me:* Specific attitudes, choices, or habits.

✦ *God:* His love, mercy, holiness, peace, joy, etc.

PRIVATE WORLD JOURNAL

I am grateful for—I praise You for—I am feeling—I am thinking—I need help with

PRIVATE WORLD DEVOTIONS (Continued)

THURSDAY: Memorize it. Take the verse with you—write it on a card or put it in your phone, iPod, or PDA. Go over it throughout the day so that it begins to *live* in your heart and mind.

FRIDAY: Pray it. Personalize the verse as you pray for yourself or for others or in praise to God. To pray is literally "to think about." Try thinking out loud or writing in your **PRIVATE WORLD JOURNAL.**

SATURDAY: Share it. Ask the Lord to bring someone to mind or in your path today who needs good news. Don't be shy—just let it out! Whether you IM, write, text, tell, or send it, the joy of God's Word will flow from your heart into theirs.

PRAYER REQUESTS

Date	Name	Need	Answer

PRIVATE WORLD JOURNAL

I am grateful for—I praise You for—I am feeling—I am thinking—I need help with

NOTES

CHAPTER 4

LEAVE ME ALONE!

BUT DOESN'T ANYBODY CARE?

KEY SCRIPTURE

*Rejoice with those who rejoice and
weep with those who weep.*

—Romans 12:15

IT COULD BE YOU!

As a young boy growing up in San Francisco, Joel Engle never knew his father. Tragedy struck one day when Joel found his mother lying on the kitchen floor after suffering a stroke. Soon after, she passed away, leaving eleven-year-old Joel in the care of his elderly grandparents.

"Life was basically miserable, and I was constantly afraid," reflects Joel. "I was consumed with thoughts of what was going to happen to me. I felt alone, unloved, and unhappy."

> *A friend loves at all times, and a brother is born for adversity.*
> **—Proverbs 17:17**

At the age of fourteen, Joel had no other option but to check himself into the local Baptist children's home. "Doesn't anybody care?" became the haunting question in his mind.

At age sixteen, Joel met some close friends of his house parents by the name of Dale and Nadine Engle. A bond was formed, and soon after, Joel not only moved in with them but also became part of their family by taking their last name. It was a landmark year for

Joel, the same year he realized that Christ was the only One who would never leave him. From then on, with his hope firmly planted, there was no looking back.

"God began to speak to me, and I longed to use my talents for Him," Joel says. "I prayed, 'God if You will give me the ability to play the piano, I will never sing a song or write a song that doesn't glorify Your name!'"

Joel had to go through a huge healing process over his growing-up years. The songs he wrote became natural expressions of how God delivered him from the wounds of the past. He says, "There are so many Christians today who live in pain secretly. I want to give hope to them by showing how God healed me."[1]

WHY KNOW IT?

✦ Boys living in a fatherless home are two to three times more likely to be involved in crime, drop out of school, and get divorced.

✦ Girls living in a fatherless home are two to three times more likely to become pregnant as teenagers and have their marriages end in divorce.[2]

transfuse (trans FYOOZ) : to cause to pass from one to another; transmit

When adversity becomes overwhelming, most people find themselves going back and forth between "Doesn't anybody care?" and "Leave me alone!" Well-meaning friends may say, "I know how you feel," but we think, *How come nobody's listening?*

The truth is that friends and relationships are essential to getting through adversity.

*Rejoice with those who rejoice and weep
with those who weep.* —**Romans 12:15**

We all know that a genuine relationship with God is the foundation of a successful Christian life. But when we're going through hard times, it helps to be able to talk to someone with skin, someone we can see face to face! God's plan is for us to help one another in difficult times.

Meeting emotional and relational needs through relationships has always been God's plan. In fact, relationships were a vital part of the earthly life of Christ. Jesus began His public ministry by calling twelve disciples, who were also His friends and traveling companions. Jesus knew there would be both joys and disappointments ahead, and He chose relationships before He began. This is a significant example to us.

Healthy relationships will impact our lives forever. To acknowledge that we have needs is not an admission of weakness; it's a realization that we are human. We need God, and we need one another. That's the way God made us. Just think: if we didn't have relational needs, we would be unaware of the people around us, and life would probably be somewhat boring.

infuse (in FYOOZ)¦ to cause to be permeated with something (as a principle or quality) that alters usually for the better

What do we need from others? When we're hurting, we know we need help, but we just don't know how to explain exactly what we are feeling. Instead of being honest about our emotions, we send out confusing signals, hoping our friends and family will interpret them correctly. We do things like:

- ✦ Slam doors and stay in our rooms;

- ✦ Yell out hateful words;

- ✦ Use offensive language;

- ✦ Withdraw and don't talk at all;

- ✦ Act out in anger;

- ✦ Act like the pain doesn't hurt;

- ✦ Laugh when we speak of serious loss;

- ✦ Withdraw from friends.

The pain you feel over your loss, discouragement, or circumstance is very real; no one in his or her right mind would deny it. But emotional damage can play for keeps if you are careless. Don't play the game of trying to punish those who have hurt you by staying angry or refusing to forgive. Before you make the wrong choices, seek out help and make the decision to get healthy again.

What negative behavior have you used to express your feelings?

How can you use positive behavior and words to express those same feelings?

While we should ultimately direct our expectations toward God, a crucial first step in trusting Him is to express our needs to others clearly and openly.

Write three sentences about difficult circumstances or negative emotions you experienced this week. How can you describe this to others in a clear way?

By communicating our needs in a loving and respectful manner, we face our fears of being let down, but we also reinforce our trust in God's faithfulness.

As you would expect, God does know our needs, and He has already given instructions to others on how to help. Don't you love that about Him?

✦ Comfort one another.

> *Blessed are those who mourn, for they shall be comforted.* —**Matthew 5:4**

To comfort is to respond to a hurting person with words, feelings, and touch; to hurt with and for another's grief or pain.

✦ Encourage one another.

> *Encourage each other and give each other strength, just as you are doing now.* —**1 Thessalonians 5:11 NCV**

To encourage is to urge another person to persist toward a goal; to inspire others toward love and good deeds (Hebrews 10:24).

The way that God intended for us to empty emotional pain from our lives is to comfort others in their pain. Pray, "Lord, use me this week to comfort and encourage someone in the halls of my school or at work or at church or in my home. Help me to look for these opportunities and to take them when they appear."

diffuse (di FYOOZ) : to pour out and permit or cause to spread freely; to extend, scatter

In addition to being relational, spiritual, and physical, part of being created in the image of God means we will be emotional at times. Showing emotion is a normal and necessary part of being created in the image of God.

When Christ was on earth, He showed emotions:

✦ In John 11:35, Jesus wept.

✦ In Matthew 21:12, Jesus was angry.

✦ In Luke 10:21, Jesus rejoiced in the Spirit.

✦ In the Garden of Gethsemane, Jesus cried out to God.

Emotions are:

✦ internal signals that publicly display to others how we are feeling;

✦ the language with which we connect with others;

✦ positive when they allow us to connect with others;

✦ negative when we shut others out or make bad choices.

Emotions Affect Our Behavior

> *But, speaking the truth in love, may
> grow up in all things into Him who is
> the head—Christ.* **—Ephesians 4:15**

Each of us needs encouragement and comfort on a daily basis. Every day, people you encounter deposit a penny, a nickel, a quarter, or more into your emotional bank. The result is a positive internal feeling of being comforted and encouraged. By walking in emotional health, you have something in the bank to make a withdrawal on in the event of a bad day or disappointing circumstance.

To *get* more emotional encouragement, you should be a contagious *giver* of encouragement. God's Word frequently tells us to invest in people in positive ways, following His lead, building one another up. God has designed us for win-win relationships in which we meet the relational needs of others, and they meet our relational needs.

In order to develop the habit of building people up, we have to consciously choose to do so. Can you think of one person in each of your classes who you can build up this week? Every day, say something nice or encouraging to that person.

Ask God to bring to mind people you don't usually see, those who might not have many friends, or those who are not easy to like because of offensive lifestyles. Who are they?

Blessed be the God and Father of our Lord Jesus Christ, the Father of mercies and God of all comfort, who comforts us in all our tribulation, that we may be able to comfort those who are in any trouble, with the comfort with which we ourselves are comforted by God. —**2 Corinthians 1:3–4**

Since we are created with needs that can only be met through relationships, every human relationship can be said to include two needy people. In healthy friendships, the focus is on giving to one another... Jesus says, "Freely you have received, freely give" (Matthew 10:8).

You can give contagiously by:

✦ Intentionally spending time listening to your friend, getting to know him or her better.

✦ Surprising your friends and relatives with unexpected phone calls, cards, or visits.

Your parents work hard to provide for you, to care for your needs, and love you as much as they love their own life. Take the time this week to write them a note of gratitude and to express your love to them. This will be a huge deposit in their emotional bank and one that will bring about a special touch in your relationship. You might want to make a note in your planner to do this once a month. What a wonderful thing gratitude is!

Decide today to be emotionally healthy and to help others to do the same. "Bear one another's burdens, and so fulfill the law of Christ" (Galatians 6:2).

Galatians 6:1 says, "Brothers and sisters, if someone in your group does something wrong, you who are spiritual should go to that person and gently help make him right again" (NCV). The Greek word translated "make him right" is a medical term meaning to put back in the socket. If someone has fallen, even if it's you, it is painful, because you are literally out of the socket or out of joint.

In any time of adversity, there is an emotional cross-road before us. Do we stand still, go backward, or move forward? The answer in God's book is always to move forward, although the pace is unique to the person and situation.

One way you can receive help in moving forward is to ask a family member or friend to help you set small, reasonable goals. These goals give you a sense of being in control, and an opportunity to work alongside your friend as you grow together through healing.

Survey the situation and consider the small steps forward listed on the chart below. Circle those that apply to you right now. What other situations and steps forward can you think of? Write them below.

Situation:	Small Step Forward:
Personal illness	Look up info on the Internet.
	Read stories of others who have gotten well.
Difficulty learning	Set up a study group.
	Ask a friend to tutor you in specific areas.
Death of loved one	Make a memory book of special times and photos.
	Set up a regular appointment to talk it through.
	Talk to someone who has also gone through this.

Situation:	Small Step Forward:
Relationship breakup	Read books about healthy emotions.
	Make new friends and expand your social circles.
	Determine to help someone else going through it.
Family conflict	Choose one nice thing to do for each family member during the week.
	Write a note of gratitude to a family member.
Lack of faith in God	Select one Scripture each week to memorize.
	Ask a prayer partner to join you once a week.
	Talk to your youth minister or teacher.

WORSHIP IN THE STORM

Life is a daily emotional battle that consists of endless pressing decisions about where to invest your time, attention, and effort. Without established goals, confusion, contradiction, and conflict can take over. By setting goals, a person faced with unhealthy emotions can look toward a healthy future, today and the next.

Setting goals allows you to show an example to others of how to move forward in difficult times. When we think through the important areas of our lives and choose what we want them to look like in the future, making plans to move in that direction, we serve as positive witnesses to others. When we ask others to join us in our emotional growth and healing, we demonstrate God's emphasis on relational community.

[FUSE BOX]

A man who has friends must himself be friendly, but there is a friend who sticks closer than a brother. —Proverbs 18:24

Worship His majesty.
—Jack Hayford

PRIVATE WORLD DEVOTIONS

MONDAY: See it. Read the surrounding passages or chapter for the Key Scripture so that you can get an understanding of the background and context. This helps you to really *see* the verse.

TUESDAY: Hear it. Read the daily Key Scripture and/or surrounding passage out loud, putting your name in, if applicable. For example, <u>John</u> *can do all things through Christ. Thieves have come to destroy* <u>John</u>, *but Jesus has come that* <u>John</u> *might have eternal life.*

WEDNESDAY: Write it. Write the verse and then what it says about:

✦ *Others:* Respond, serve, and love as Jesus would.

✦ *Me:* Specific attitudes, choices, or habits.

✦ *God:* His love, mercy, holiness, peace, joy, etc.

PRIVATE WORLD JOURNAL

I am grateful for—I praise You for—I am feeling—I am thinking—I need help with

PRIVATE WORLD DEVOTIONS *(Continued)*

THURSDAY: Memorize it. Take the verse with you—write it on a card or put it in your phone, iPod, or PDA. Go over it throughout the day so that it begins to *live* in your heart and mind.

FRIDAY: Pray it. Personalize the verse as you pray for yourself or for others or in praise to God. To pray is literally "to think about." Try thinking out loud or writing in your **PRIVATE WORLD JOURNAL.**

SATURDAY: Share it. Ask the Lord to bring someone to mind or in your path today who needs good news. Don't be shy—just let it out! Whether you IM, write, text, tell, or send it, the joy of God's Word will flow from your heart into theirs.

PRAYER REQUESTS

Date	Name	Need	Answer

PRIVATE WORLD JOURNAL

I am grateful for—I praise You for—I am feeling—I am thinking—I need help with

NOTES

CHAPTER 5

THIS STUFF IS TOO HARD

WHY AM I SO STRESSED?

KEY SCRIPTURE

*I can do all things through Christ
who strengthens me.*
—Philippians 4:13

IT COULD BE YOU!

Which of these have you dealt with recently?

✦ A friend who bailed on helping with a school project

✦ A really tough test or assignment

✦ Balancing schoolwork, personal responsibility, and after-school activities

✦ Disappointment in a friend or relationship

✦ Piles of assignments

✦ Family conflict

✦ Illness or feeling tired

✦ Information overload

That's why we all crave entertainment, rest, diversion. These all fall under the category of *recreation*, which literally means to *re-create* your inner being.

If you chose any of the above, congratulations! You are a normal teenager. Stress is a part of your life.

WHY KNOW IT?

✦ One third of U.S. teens say they feel stressed-out on a daily basis.[1]

✦ Fifty-three percent of teens who are involved with a boyfriend or a girlfriend say their relationship causes them stress.[2]

transfuse (trans FYOOZ): to cause to pass from one to another; transmit

Stress is actually an engineering term that describes stress or strain on a bridge or building. It starts as a crack, but if left unattended can cause the entire structure to collapse. These same types of "stress fractures" appear in humans. The everyday stresses and strains of life build up in us and, if we don't attend to them, they can cause spiritual, emotional, and physical breakdown.

Eustress is good or positive stress—such as making new friends, doing well in school, new opportunities.

Distress is bad or negative stress—such as difficult people, death or illness, relationship conflicts.

Hear me when I call, O God of my righteousness! You have relieved me in my distress; have mercy on me, and hear my prayer. How long, O you sons of men, will you turn my glory to shame? How long will you love worthlessness and seek falsehood? Selah.

*But know that the L*ORD *has set apart for Himself him who is godly; the L*ORD *will hear when I call to Him. Be angry, and do not sin. Meditate within your heart on your bed, and be still. Selah.*

Offer the sacrifices of righteousness, and put your trust in the Lord. **—Psalm 4:1–5**

Psalm 4 is called the "Evening Psalm." Before going to sleep, David prayed and sorted out the stress and emotions of the day.

◆ What a great habit to develop.

◆ What a healthy habit to choose.

The body and mind were meant to *process emotions*, not just be *surrounded* with them.

infuse (in FYOOZ), to cause to be permeated with something (as a principle or quality) that alters usually for the better

Hear me when I call, O God of my righteousness! You have relieved me in my distress; have mercy on me, and hear my prayer. **—Psalm 4:1**

David called out to God about the *distress* in his life. He paints the picture here of hiding in a very small space, like a cave, from the enemy. And, suddenly, God *relieves* him by giving David some space emotionally and spiritually, some room to breathe.

Have you ever felt like that—like everything is crowding in on you? This probably causes you to overreact about nothing—you just need some space!

What are some things you might have overreacted to recently? Select from the list, and write about the specific incident. Was your reaction justified, or do you think you overreacted because of other stresses?

+ Your parents' rules

+ Calls (or lack of calls) from friends

+ Advice from teachers

+ Homework pressures

+ The way someone talked to you

+ Grades

+ Other

Do you sometimes feel like you can't breathe, can't sleep, can't think, because all of the demands on your emotions are more than you can handle? God understands.

David was praying for ways to *cope* with stress. "Hear me," he cried out. God does listen to us, but He also encourages us to look at the *source* of that stress in order to change or eliminate the pressure we are feeling.

David begins to pour out his heart over the source of his stresses with two questions to the enemies who are pursuing him:

"How long, O you sons of men, will you turn my glory to shame? How long will you love worthlessness and seek falsehood?" (Psalm 4:2).

Question 1: How long will you turn my glory to shame?

David had worked hard and endured much to stand as a man of God. Now, his reputation was on the line as enemies in the land sought to kill him physically and destroy him emotionally and spiritually.

Have you ever felt like this?

✦ You try so hard at school to stand as a Christian for the right things, and yet there are those who seek to discredit you?

✦ You work to be a leader in your youth group and someone has hurt your feelings or spoken ill of your efforts?

✦ Do you ever find yourself saying, "I can't do anything right?"

This is how David felt as he hid in the cave, and the result was distress and discouragement.

God understands how you feel because His greatness and unconditional love are often misunderstood, misquoted, and unappreciated.

The culture sometimes takes His great *glory*—as Creator and Savior—and turns it into *shame*.

If we are not guilty, those of us who have trusted Him as Savior can sometimes do the same. "Never!" you say? How about this:

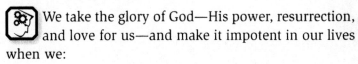 We take the glory of God—His power, resurrection, and love for us—and make it impotent in our lives when we:

✦ allow our choices to be dictated by the crowd;

✦ make decisions based on emotional need instead of commitment to moral excellence;

- ✦ worry and fret instead of believe in His power and love for us;

- ✦ settle for second best in our lives because excellence is "too hard";

- ✦ doubt God because of difficult circumstances;

- ✦ use "I can't help it" as an excuse.

GROUP DISCUSSION

Select one of the above and discuss a scenario where we forget God's power because of preoccupation with stress, crowd control pressure, or circumstances.

Question 2: How long will you love worthlessness and seek falsehood?
In David's day, idol worship was as common as catching a cold. The idols were lifeless, stone statues that could offer nothing in reality, but were superstitiously believed in. They were falsehoods.

You probably don't worship stone gods, but you might still be seeking falsehood in other ways.

 We allow worthless, false influences to rule us when we . . .

Allow what others say to influence how we think about:

- ✦ ourselves

- ✦ God

- ✦ the friends we choose

- ✦ how we make decisions

- ✦ our definition of sin

- ✦ moral values

Allow unfinished emotional business to go on:

✦ dreams we're afraid to start

✦ friends we don't forgive

✦ habits we don't control

✦ relationship issues we need to sort out, but don't

We can rise above the stress of everyday life when we remember who God is and where our strength comes from.

Put your name in the blank:

_____ *can do all things through Christ who strengthens me.* **—Philippians 4:13**

diffuse (di FYOOZ); to pour out and permit or cause to spread freely; to extend, scatter

As a young boy, David fought wild animals that attacked his sheep.

As a teen, he slew the giant who defied his God and harassed his nation.

As a young adult, he was threatened by Saul, the most powerful man politically in his world.

Every day, in all times of your life, you will face and fight enemies, such as:

✦ Satan, who tempts and twists your way; and

✦ yourself, as you put yourself into situations that you should run from.

The Lord was with David every step of the way.

And the Lord is with you.

What is one challenge you are facing: a temptation, a difficult person, a learning struggle, a relationship problem?

> You will never
> find time for anything.
> If you want time, you
> must take it.
> —Charles Buxton

Are you merely *coping* with the issue, or are you *getting to the source* of the issue?

What is ONE THING you can do this week to begin to resolve the conflict issue?

THINK ABOUT IT!

At the end of verse 2, the psalmist adds a very important word, *selah*, which means "think about it!"

Selah meaning "pause, reflection", within the context of a prayer or psalms, is similar in purpose to Amen in that it stresses the importance of the preceding passage.

In this way, *selah* is thought to imply that one should pause and reflect on what has been said.[3]

One of the greatest hindrances to peace in our lives is not making time for positive habits and peaceful thoughts. God wants you to enjoy life as a grand adventure with Him, but you must take some control over the areas of life that are robbing you of the power of His glory and of a peaceful heart.

Set Apart for God

> *But know that the Lord has set apart for Himself him who is godly; the Lord will hear when I call to Him.* —**Psalm 4:3**

What a wonderful phrase—"the Lord has set us apart for Himself!" It's an intimate phrase, indicating a close, personal relationship. The one who has a godly heart, who comes away from the noise and confusion of the day, is *set apart* into a special time with God.

The student who is *set apart* for godliness has a quiet center:

- ✦ Turn off music, TV, Internet, telephones for at least one hour.

- ✦ Spend time processing emotions at the end of the day.

Inspiration gets you started; habits take you across the finish line.

- ✦ Have a genuine quiet time alone with God, reading the Scripture, listening to or singing praise songs, praying through problems and needs.

- ✦ Develop the habit of journaling thoughts.

- ✦ Spend time planning and organizing your life.

- ✦ Use a planner, every day. Don't try to keep information, times, places in your head. There's just not enough room! The average person will see one thousand pieces of information in an hour.[4]

- ✦ Honor commitments such as studying, friendships, families, organizing life, and spending time with the Lord.

- ✦ Be a problem-solver more than a complainer.

- ✦ Think through difficulty rather than giving up on it.

- ✦ Make health a priority.

- ✦ Eat healthy foods to give energy.

- ✦ Go to bed at least twenty minutes earlier, improving sleep habits.

- ✦ Exercise.

- ✦ Spend time with people who care (family and good friends) and don't stress about those who don't.

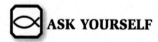

ASK YOURSELF

Did my choices last week lead me to where I want to go in life?

_____

_____

_____

Am I *set apart* differently from everyone else, or am I just like the average teen?

Am I working through stress? Am I taking time to organize my thoughts? Do I have a regular "evening psalm" routine?

David moves from the *source* of his stress to daily habits that will eliminate his stress. In other words, start making some positive changes in your life to combat those stresses you can control.

What ONE CHANGE can I make this week to begin a life of being *set apart* to Christ?

Selah!

> *Be angry, and do not sin. Meditate within your heart on your bed, and be still. Selah*
>
> *Offer the sacrifices of righteousness.*
> **—Psalm 4:4–5**

Let's unpack this verse.

Be angry, and do not sin.

What? Is this even possible? Yes! There are two types of anger:

Righteous anger is good anger—it causes us to set things right, to declare truth.

Unrighteous anger is bad anger—it is reactive and gives birth to more anger.

There are two ways to deal with conflict:

✦ You can *react to the situation.* "**My** feelings were hurt. **I** was embarrassed. You were mean to **me. I'm** so mad!"

✦ You can *respond to the situation.* "What happened here? What's the solution? Did I offend you? I'm sorry. How do we improve this or keep it from happening again?"

Think about a recent conflict or argument with a family member, friend, coworker, or teammate. What was the conflict about?

_____

_____

_____

Did you react or respond?

_____

_____

_____

If it were to come up again, how would you handle it?

Once again, it comes down to *choice*.

. . . Meditate within your heart on your bed, and be still . . .

Remember that this is one of David's *evening psalms*. At the end of the day, David knew it was valuable to:

✦ clear out emotions,

✦ rehearse the greatness and power of God, and

✦ be quiet enough to hear the Lord speak.

. . . Offer the sacrifices of righteousness . . .

Have you ever thought, "I wish I could offer a sacrifice to God. But what does that mean? How do I do that?"

> "We shape our habits, and our habits shape us."
> —Hyrum Smith

The word *sacrifice* means "to be, to remain so," and one of the greatest gifts we can offer to the Lord is a life that "remains so."

Cultivate the habit of asking yourself:

✦ Is this choice in line with my moral values, my highest priorities?

✦ Is this choice one I would want others to emulate?

+ Does this choice take me on a path toward my future goals?

+ What regrets might I have?

+ What are the benefits to others?

GROUP DISCUSSION

Go over the information on stress below and discuss whether the statements are true or false. Give specific examples.

Stress, if not dealt with can cause you to:

+ Blow up when you don't mean to;

+ Lose concentration on important projects;

+ Make bad decisions out of frustration;

+ Leave you feeling out of control and hopeless.

WORSHIP IN THE STORM

Put your trust in the Lord. —**Psalm 4:5**

At the end of a long day of hiding from an evil and dangerous enemy, David ends with a simple, but profound truth: "Put your trust in the Lord."

The Hebrew word translated "trust" in this verse means to be confident and sure! Put your name in the blank below and say this prayer often during your evening time of quiet:

I, _____ , put my *confidence* in the Lord. I, _____, am sure of His greatness, power, and love for me.

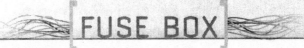

[FUSE BOX]

Be sure, be confident in this: The Lord loves me intensely. He wants the best for my life!

> Worship is a lifestyle. Embrace God fully and let him embrace you. Don't be afraid to be washed in heaven's rain.
> —Michael W. Smith

PRIVATE WORLD DEVOTIONS

MONDAY: See it. Read the surrounding passages or chapter for the Key Scripture so that you can get an understanding of the background and context. This helps you to really *see* the verse.

TUESDAY: Hear it. Read the daily Key Scripture and/or surrounding passage out loud, putting your name in, if applicable. For example, <u>John</u> *can do all things through Christ. Thieves have come to destroy* <u>John</u>, *but Jesus has come that* <u>John</u> *might have eternal life.*

WEDNESDAY: Write it. Write the verse and then what it says about:

✦ *Others:* Respond, serve, and love as Jesus would.

✦ *Me:* Specific attitudes, choices, or habits.

✦ *God:* His love, mercy, holiness, peace, joy, etc.

PRIVATE WORLD JOURNAL

I am grateful for—I praise You for—I am feeling—I am thinking—I need help with

PRIVATE WORLD DEVOTIONS (Continued)

THURSDAY: Memorize it. Take the verse with you—write it on a card or put it in your phone, iPod, or PDA. Go over it throughout the day so that it begins to *live* in your heart and mind.

FRIDAY: Pray it. Personalize the verse as you pray for yourself or for others or in praise to God. To pray is literally "to think about." Try thinking out loud or writing in your **PRIVATE WORLD JOURNAL.**

SATURDAY: Share it. Ask the Lord to bring someone to mind or in your path today who needs good news. Don't be shy—just let it out! Whether you IM, write, text, tell, or send it, the joy of God's Word will flow from your heart into theirs.

PRAYER REQUESTS

Date	Name	Need	Answer

PRIVATE WORLD JOURNAL

I am grateful for—I praise You for—I am feeling—I am thinking—I need help with

NOTES

CHAPTER 6

THE ADVERSITY OF NO CHOICE

WHAT DOES GOD WANT FROM ME?

KEY SCRIPTURE

And He was withdrawn from them about a stone's throw, and He knelt down and prayed, saying, "Father, if it is Your will, take this cup away from Me; nevertheless not My will, but Yours, be done."
—Luke 22:41, 42

IT COULD BE YOU!

David Nasser remembers going to military school in Iran at the age of nine and being called to a school assembly. His name was called, and he went to the front, where a soldier pulled out a gun and pointed it at him. As David was shaking in fear, the soldier said, "I'm about to kill you right now." The principal got between David and the gun and told David to go home and not to come back.

David explains, "What I did not understand at that time was that my country, Iran, was going through a revolution. Through a series of events, my family escaped and landed in the U.S. We moved into the neighborhood right at the time when Iran was taking Americans hostage, and because we were Iranian, we instantly became outcasts. This rejection continued for years. Once I reached high school, I took my brain, put it on the top shelf, and said to the world, 'You find my identity for me. Tell me what clothes to wear, which friends to choose, what kind of language to use . . . I'm just tired of feeling insignificant.' One guy kept inviting me to church, but I could not understand that people could just love you because they loved someone named Jesus. Eventually people in that church loved me into salvation. My testimony is not about some Iranian kid who escaped. My testimony is about a church who loved somebody who was different."

David Nasser lived through the adversity of no choice. He had done nothing to warrant the pain he endured as a child and could do nothing to keep the pain from coming. But God was there, working in his life and working things for his good, just as He will do for you.

WHY KNOW IT?

♦ An estimated 100,000 students were displaced from their homes and moved to schools in other states and cities after Hurricane Katrina.[1]

♦ Thirteen million children and teens are internally displaced because of war, and two hundred and fifty thousand are child soldiers.[2]

transfuse (trans FYOOZ) : to cause to pass from one to another; transmit

The adversity of no choice comes to us in a whirlwind. Sometimes there are storm warnings—we know it's on the way because of impending circumstances or the choices of others that affect us. Other times, a gentle breeze is blowing in our lives one minute and a tropical storm drops in the next. It is in these times of *no choice* that we learn to surrender to God's will and to "the peace of God, which surpasses all understanding" (Philippians 4:7).

*Then they came to a place which was named Gethsemane; and He said to His disciples, "Sit here while I pray." And He took Peter, James, and John with Him, and He began to be troubled and deeply distressed. Then He said to them, "My soul is exceedingly sorrowful, even to death. Stay here and watch." He went a little farther, and fell on the ground, and prayed that if it were possible, the hour might pass from Him. And He said, "Abba, Father, all things are possible for You. Take this cup away from Me; nevertheless, not what I will, but what You will." —***Mark 14:32–36**

Peter faced adversity of choice at the same time that Jesus faced the adversity of *no choice*. While Peter slept, Jesus went to the Father with fear and trembling about the difficulty ahead:

Jesus was fully aware of the betrayal, beatings, and the cross ahead. This storm was easy to spot for it had been foretold by the prophets hundreds of years earlier. He had read the Scriptures. He knew the pain that was to come.

In this darkest hour of His life, He turned to both man and God. "And He took Peter, James, and John with Him, and He began to be troubled and deeply distressed. Then He said to them, "My soul is exceedingly sorrowful, even to death. Stay here and watch" (Mark 14:33–34). But His disciples, even with the best of intentions, let Him down.

The Father did not.

We have discussed in other chapters that man needs relationships with others. Jesus was no exception, and

He began this horrible task by meeting with His disciples.

infuse (in FYOOZ) : to cause to be permeated with something (as a principle or quality) that alters usually for the better

Jesus prepared His disciples for the storm ahead, and He prepared Himself for the horrors He would endure.

Prepare for the Storm through Fellowship

> *And He sent Peter and John, saying, "Go and*
> *prepare the Passover for us, that we may eat."*
> *. . . So they went and found it just as He*
> *had said to them, and they prepared the*
> *Passover. When the hour had come, He sat*
> *down, and the twelve apostles with Him.*
> *Then He said to them, "With fervent desire*
> *I have desired to eat this Passover with*
> *you before I suffer.* **—Luke 22:8–15**

Jesus thought of everything, even down to a time together where they would eat a meal, pray together, and sing a hymn of praise. *Selah!* The Greek text explains that He *craved* this time with His friends;[3] He needed it for His spirit as He was about to go from health to great suffering.

If you know that you are going to face a difficult situation, get together first with your friends as Jesus did. Share, pray, sing, and worship God, just as Jesus did.

Do you have the kind of friendships that you can count on when a storm is about to hit? People who will pray with you, love you, and walk through the difficult days? If so, who are they?

What can you do to strengthen these friendships; to encourage each of them?

_____

_____

_____

> *Then they came to a place which was named Gethsemane; and He said to His disciples, "Sit here while I pray." And He took Peter, James, and John with Him, and He began to be troubled and deeply distressed. Then He said to them, "My soul is exceedingly sorrowful, even to death. Stay here and watch."* —**Mark 14:32–34**

To describe the sorrow Jesus felt is difficult. We can write it, but we can only imagine the depth of the pain He felt as He was about to experience isolation from God and man. Jesus' pain has been described as "the most shocking amazement, mingled with grief; surrounded with sorrow on every side, breaking in upon him with such violence, as was ready to separate his soul from his body."[4]

> To reflect on the personal care of God is to find strength to go forward in times of adversity.

Why such horrible pain? Get this: It wasn't the horrors of the physical pain that was the most frightening for the Lord Jesus. It was the spiritual judgment He was about to witness, the betrayal of friendships so dear, and the pain of watching people He so dearly loved turned against God. Commentator John Gill says, "The sight of all the sins of his people coming upon him; at the black storm of wrath, that was gathering thick over him; at the sword of justice which was brandished against him; and at the curses of the righteous law, which, like so many thunderbolts of vengeance, were directed at him."[5]

Jesus knew He was about to take on the sins of the world, so He prepared for the storm by bringing His friends.

Think about the adversity you have experienced in the past or are currently going through. Does Jesus understand your pain? Do you think He understands the depth of your emotions and how hard this is for you? What do you base that on?

Prepare for the Storm Through Prayer

> *And He was withdrawn from them about a stone's throw, and He knelt down and prayed, saying, "Father, if it is Your will, take this cup away from Me; nevertheless not My will, but Yours, be done." Then an angel appeared to Him from heaven, strengthening Him.* —**Luke 22:41–43**

The time of preparation with friends had been a good time, but now Jesus must wrestle alone with God as He prepares to take on the sins of the world. All of the questions that you have asked, He also asked: "Why me? Why now? Do I have to do this? Isn't there another way?"

If Jesus ever gave us a command He could not enable us to fulfill, He would be a liar; and if we are to make our inability a barrier to obedience, it means we are telling God there is something He has not taken into account.

God did not answer Jesus' prayer by changing the circumstances. The storm was coming, and Jesus had to prepare to endure the suffering of the cross.

God Will Meet You There

We have seen over and over in Scripture that in times of adversity, Jesus will meet you there. He came to the disciples in the storm, He was with Paul in prison, and He will come to you.

Jesus prayed, "This is My will—take this cup away. But I want Your will, God." When He made this final declaration of surrender, God ministered to Him by sending an angel to strengthen Him (Luke 22:43). God still sends angels to minister to us (Hebrews 13:2), people around us every day who encourage us, if we let them.

The key to the strength and presence of God in any adversity is *surrender*. In times of adversity, we can pray, like Jesus did, "Not my will, but Yours, be done."

What do you need to do to come to the place of surrender? This is such a personal and private time with God, but here today, pray quietly as a group for the faith to surrender to God's will.

ASK YOURSELF

Am I ready to make this declaration for everyday life as well as adversity?

diffuse (di FYOOZ) : to pour out and permit or cause to spread freely; to extend, scatter

Power in Surrender

> *Then He came the third time and said to them,*
> *"Are you still sleeping and resting? It is enough!*
> *The hour has come; behold, the Son of Man*
> *is being betrayed into the hands of sinners.*
> *Rise, let us be going.* **—Mark 14:41–42**

As soon as He surrendered to the will of God, an angel came and ministered to Him. The resulting power was enough to make Him stand up and begin the task ahead. It would have been easy for Him to give up when He saw that His friends were still asleep, still oblivious to what

He was about to do, but He didn't, probably because He understood how much God loved Him.

Notice Jesus' definitive command: "Rise, let us be going" (v. 42). On His knees there in the garden, as Jesus prayed, the angel of God very likely pulled back the curtain of the future and showed Him the glory of the resurrection and of His reign in heaven. He saw that God would take the pain and make it very good.

 There comes a time in every adversity when we, too, must rise from our knees and move forward just as Jesus did. As you pray through your adversity, keep repeating that phrase in your heart: *Rise, let us be going.* As you do, God will prepare you to go forward as you are strengthened and ready, as Jesus is ready to move you.

Rise—Get up from the circumstances.

What circumstances in your life right now do you rise above? Write them here:

_____

_____

_____

> We shall draw from the heart of suffering itself the means of inspiration and survival.
> —Sir Winston Churchill
>   (1874–1965)

Let us be going—What is ONE THING you can begin to accomplish toward a goal this week that will move you forward in life?

Power in the Promises

We have been given this same promise: "All things work together for good to those who love God, to those who are the called according to His purpose" (Romans 8:28). This promise is best understood by what it does *not* say.

It *does not* say that all things work together for:

✦ our comfort, convenience, or our popularity.

✦ a balance between painful childhood and the rest of life as a pleasure cruise.

It *does* say that all things work together "for good." That refers to the *big picture*—that is, our salvation and our relationship to the Father.

As Paul writes this verse to us, he has endured beatings, shipwrecks, and betrayals of the most serious nature. Yet he writes with certainty that *we know* God will do good.

How does he *know* this? Because Paul knew the resurrection as a powerful truth.

 Tony Campolo wrote a book called *It's Friday, But Sunday's Coming*. The book is built around Good

Friday, the pain of the crucifixion, and the fact that on Easter Sunday, the good news of Jesus' resurrection followed. That may be the simplest, most powerful definition of Romans 8:28: that in every *cross*, God will bring a *resurrection*. He will work *all things* for good in our lives.

He did not say how or when. He just said that "all things work together for good" for those of us who have experienced both the cross and the resurrection in our lives.

Can you pray this prayer today? "Lord, You know my heart and the hurts I face. Thank You for loving me in this time, and for walking alongside me. Today I trust You to bring about good from this pain. I will not ask when or how, but I will believe that Resurrection Sunday is coming in my life."

A rainbow's visible colors are always arrayed in the same order: red, orange, yellow, green, blue, indigo, and violet. God's promise to you is that you will go through storms of different sizes, but in the end a rainbow of promises will be yours, if you will believe.

There is great power in believing that God intensely loves you. Because you know this to be true, then you can believe that He will work all things together for good, and you can confidently pass this truth on to others, even this week.

WORSHIP IN THE STORM

The key to facing heartache and difficulty victoriously is knowing that God is in control of your life and circumstances. He knows exactly what you are facing. He knew what Jesus would endure on the cross, and He knows what you face.

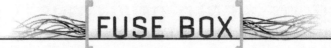

FUSE BOX

Each person whom God uses greatly will face times of suffering—dark times that challenge their faith.

PRIVATE WORLD DEVOTIONS

MONDAY: See it. Read the surrounding passages or chapter for the Key Scripture so that you can get an understanding of the background and context. This helps you to really *see* the verse.

TUESDAY: Hear it. Read the daily Key Scripture and/or surrounding passage out loud, putting your name in, if applicable. For example, <u>John</u> *can do all things through Christ. Thieves have come to destroy* <u>John</u>, *but Jesus has come that* <u>John</u> *might have eternal life.*

WEDNESDAY: Write it. Write the verse and then what it says about:

✦ *Others:* Respond, serve, and love as Jesus would.

✦ *Me:* Specific attitudes, choices, or habits.

✦ *God:* His love, mercy, holiness, peace, joy, etc.

PRIVATE WORLD JOURNAL

I am grateful for—I praise You for—I am feeling—I am thinking—I need help with

PRIVATE WORLD DEVOTIONS *(Continued)*

THURSDAY: Memorize it. Take the verse with you—write it on a card or put it in your phone, iPod, or PDA. Go over it throughout the day so that it begins to *live* in your heart and mind.

FRIDAY: Pray it. Personalize the verse as you pray for yourself or for others or in praise to God. To pray is literally "to think about." Try thinking out loud or writing in your **PRIVATE WORLD JOURNAL.**

SATURDAY: Share it. Ask the Lord to bring someone to mind or in your path today who needs good news. Don't be shy—just let it out! Whether you IM, write, text, tell, or send it, the joy of God's Word will flow from your heart into theirs.

PRAYER REQUESTS

Date	Name	Need	Answer

PRIVATE WORLD JOURNAL

I am grateful for—I praise You for—I am feeling—I am thinking—I need help with

NOTES

CHAPTER 7

THE ADVERSITY OF BAD CHOICES

WHY DID I DO THAT?

KEY SCRIPTURE

But sanctify the Lord God in your hearts, and always be ready to give a defense to everyone who asks you a reason for the hope that is in you, with meekness and fear.

—1 Peter 3:15

IT COULD BE YOU!

Tina knew better. She grew up in the church, learning the truth of God's Word as a child. But when she became a teen, she didn't fit in with the cliques that had formed in her youth group. School, however, was just the opposite, and Tina found she could be popular by being a party girl. It started small—a few drinks, a joint here and there—but her lifestyle grew too big to handle very quickly.

Tina fell in love, or at least she thought she was in love. This guy said he would marry her, and she was so excited about it. No one else she knew in high school had a marriage proposal, and she was under the spell of her supposed "fiancé." At the age of sixteen, he convinced her to try cocaine, and she became addicted. Soon she found she was pregnant, and the "fiancé" quickly disappeared. Tina's baby was born addicted to cocaine and taken from her at birth.

For Tina, the progression of sin led to adversity of choice. It was a long battle to get clean, get custody of her child, and to regain a walk with God. Today, she leads a Bible study group and shares her story with anyone who will listen. God is using her adversity to encourage Christians and show the power of salvation to many.

WHY KNOW IT?

✦ Over eight hundred thousand teens become pregnant each year.[1]

✦ The average age of those who try marijuana for the first time is 14.[2]

transfuse (trans FYOOZ): to cause to pass from one to another; transmit

In the story of Jesus at Gethsemane, two very different adversities are discussed: the adversity that comes as a result of wrong choices, and the adversity in which we have no choice. Both types of adversity are painful; both have powerful results for our lives.

Peter was the recipient of adversity of choice. He learned firsthand that God can use our response to adversity to establish a triumphant testimony to future generations, and his writings (1 and 2 Peter) speak of hope, wisdom, and encouragement to all who read them.

And when they had sung a hymn, they went out to the Mount of Olives. Then Jesus said to them, "All of you will be made to stumble because of Me this night, for it is written: 'I will strike the Shepherd, And the sheep will be

scattered.' But after I have been raised, I will go before you to Galilee." Peter said to Him, "Even if all are made to stumble, yet I will not be." Jesus said to him, "Assuredly, I say to you that today, even this night, before the rooster crows twice, you will deny Me three times." But he spoke more vehemently, "If I have to die with You, I will not deny You!" And they all said likewise. —**Mark 14:27–31**

Notice the background setting of this story. (Always check that out in any Scripture reading. The more you know about the background, the more important and alive the verse becomes in your life.)

In this case, Jesus had just completed an intimate meal with His disciples. They ate together, prayed together, and finally, sang a hymn together. Can you imagine how awesome that must have been? Singing praise and worship with the Savior? Selah! ("Think about it!") Everyone was on a spiritual high, and Peter, in particular, was ready to take on the world! Ever felt like that—after a praise service or at a youth camp, maybe?

In the midst of this "high," Jesus warned Peter, "You will be made to stumble because of Me this night."

The Greeks were famous for painting word pictures, and this verse gives us a clear example of this. The word used for *stumble* is *skandalizein*. It was from the word *skandalon* which was a picture of

> "The longer I live, the more I realize the impact of attitude on life. Attitude, to me is more important than education, than money, than circumstances, than failures, than successes, than appearance, giftedness or skill. . . . I am convinced that life is 10% of what happens to me and 90% how I react to it. And so it is with you. We are in charge of our attitudes."
> —Charles Swindoll

bait in a trap, the stick on which the animal was lured and which snapped the trap when the animal stepped on it.[3] Jesus uses the word to warn Peter about what's to come. But Peter, still in his spiritual and emotional high, protests, says, "No way—it won't happen to me."

But let's look at what happened to Peter that night:

> And they led Jesus away to the high priest; and with him were assembled all the chief priests, the elders, and the scribes. But Peter followed Him at a distance, right into the courtyard of the high priest. And he sat with the servants and warmed himself at the fire. Now as Peter was below in the courtyard, one of the servant girls of the high priest came. And when she saw Peter warming himself, she looked at him and said, "You also were with Jesus of Nazareth." But he denied it, saying, "I neither know nor understand what you are saying." And he went out on the porch, and a rooster crowed. And the servant girl saw him again, and began to say to those who stood by, "This is one of them." But he denied it again. And a little later those who stood by said to Peter again, "Surely you are one of them; for you are a Galilean, and your speech shows it." Then he began to curse and swear, "I do not know this Man of whom you speak!" A second time the rooster crowed. Then Peter called to mind the word that Jesus had said to him, "Before the rooster crows twice, you will deny Me three times." And when he thought about it, he wept. —**Mark 14:53–54, 66–72**

GROUP DISCUSSION

Has this ever happened to you?

✦ You come out of church and *bam!* someone starts to speak of sexual temptation, and you stop to listen when you should leave.

✦ You come home from youth camp exhilarated and pumped only to get into an argument with your parents or best friend.

✦ You come from Bible study right into the crowd and change colors as fast as a chameleon.

Think about it: why does this spiritual metamorphosis take place when we least expect it?

---

infuse (in FYOOZ)' to cause to be permeated with something (as a principle or quality) that alters usually for the better

Progression of a Spiritual Decline

The day began with intimate fellowship, dinner, prayer, and praise songs. What could be better? What could be more fulfilling? But as evening progressed, so did the darkness progress in Peter's heart.

1. *He began with deep, genuine faith.* Peter, on an emotional and spiritual high, walked in an intimate relationship with Jesus: "And when they had sung a hymn, they went out to the Mount of Olives" (Mark 14:26).

2. *Then Peter's overconfidence took over.* He relied on his own power and pride instead of following the will of God. "If I have to die with You, I will not deny You!" (Mark 14:31). In other words, "It won't happen to me."

 Ever heard or said this before?

Each of us has times in our lives when we try to "Fly solo"—that is, we spend less and less time in the Word and rely on our own strength to stay morally pure. Not only does this *not* work, but we lose joy in our lives as we fight the culture in our own strength.

3. *His overconfidence made him spiritually lazy.* Jesus tried to warn Peter. He said, "My soul is exceedingly sorrowful, even to death. Stay here and watch" (Mark 14:34). Peter wouldn't listen, and he slept while Jesus wept in an intense time of prayer. "Then He came and found them sleeping, and said to Peter, 'Simon, are you sleeping? Could you not watch one hour?'" (Mark 14:37).

Because we are sinners by nature, we can never let down our guard in the fight against temptation. When we become spiritually lazy, our guard is down, and we easily fall into sin. What are some things you can do to stay *on guard?*

List three:

✦ _____

✦ _____

✦ _____

4. *He completely gave up his guard.* Jesus told Peter, "Watch and pray, lest you enter into temptation. The spirit indeed is willing, but the flesh is weak" (Mark 14:38). Jesus tells Peter to watch out for the trap, but Peter continues to sleep.

5. *He reacted in anger.* When adversity came in the form of soldiers and the arrest of Jesus, Peter reacted violently. He "drew his sword and struck the servant of the high priest, and cut off his ear" (Mark 14:47).

Jesus faced adversity head-on. He knew the enemy would come, He knew He had to go to the cross, and He would not allow Peter's anger. In fact, Luke tells us that Jesus put the ear back on and healed the man! Jesus loved His enemies and wants us to do the same.

Think of someone who makes life difficult for you—perhaps through criticism, betrayal, deceit, or just plain rudeness. How can you face that adversity as Jesus did? Take a moment now to pray for that person.

What is ONE THING you could do as a nice gesture for that person?

6. Peter's *intimate relationship with Jesus was replaced* . . .

✦ With a *distant following*. "But Peter followed Him at a distance, right into the courtyard of the high priest" (Mark 14:54).

✦ With *keeping company with the enemy*. "He [Peter] sat with the servants and warmed himself at the fire" (Mark 14:54).

✦ With *denial of the Savior*. "He [Peter] began to curse and swear, 'I do not know this Man of whom you speak!" (Mark 14:71).

The denial of Jesus by Peter was a progression of the heart just as any sinful choice is. It is not enough to walk about on a spiritual high, depending on spiritual experiences. We have to remember the warning of Jesus and watch out for the trap that Satan has set for us.

diffuse (di FYOOZ): to pour out and permit or cause to spread freely; to extend, scatter

Peter's adversity followed three choices or traps set before him.

1. First, it was a small test—*just one person*. He only needed enough courage to say to one servant girl, "I do know Jesus." And when she saw Peter warming himself, she looked at him and said, "You also were with Jesus of Nazareth" (Mark 14:67). But he denied it.

2. Second, he had the chance to tell *a few people*, "I believe in Jesus," but he denied it again. "And the servant girl saw him again, and began to say to those who stood by, 'This is one of them.'" (Mark 14:69). But Peter denied it again.

3. Third, he had time to *reconsider his choices* but failed. "And a little later those who stood by said to Peter again, 'Surely you are one of them; for you are a Galilean, and your speech shows it'" (Mark 14:70).

By this time, he had denied Jesus three times, and the third time he did so with anger and cursing: "Then he began to curse and swear, 'I do not know this Man of whom you speak!'" (Mark 14:71).

As Christian leaders, we must be on our guard at all times and pass the tempter's test on the first go-round, because the second and third tests will be more difficult. If you are to influence others, what are some decisions you need to make, based on Peter's choices?

GROUP DISCUSSION

Which of these do you think is important in guarding your mind and heart on a daily basis?

+ Follow Christ closely.

+ Guard and stay awake when temptation is nearby.

+ Don't sit with the enemy.

+ When Jesus calls you to prayer, *pray!*

+ Always be ready with your answer about Christ and His Word.

Notice that Peter no longer called Jesus "Lord," but just "this Man." What a sad progression of events.

> *Then Peter called to mind the word that Jesus had said to him, "Before the rooster crows twice, you will deny Me three times." And when he thought about it, he wept.* —**Mark 14:72**

Like most of us, once Peter had time to think about what he had done, he was sad and began to suffer the consequence of his choice—that is, spiritual emptiness and discouragement.

How can a person go from intimacy with Jesus, a spiritual high, to flat-out denial, and then to depression? The progression leads to spiritual weakness and an adversity of choice, the wrong choice.

✦ A spiritually weak Peter ran away rather than face the pain.

✦ Anger, shame, guilt, and finally, isolation followed as Peter could no longer face those friends who loved him.

But sanctify the Lord God in your hearts, and always be ready to give a defense to everyone who asks you a reason for the hope that is in you, with meekness and fear. —**1 Peter 3:15**

Do you think Peter is speaking from personal experience when he writes these words in the Scripture? What do you think he means when he urges us to "sanctify the Lord God in your hearts?"

The Christian leader who is *called to stand* is always ready to give a reason for his hope in Christ.

Restoration Is Good News

But there is also good news about this adversity of choice. Not only does Jesus forgive us, but He restores us to intimacy with Him again.

Wow! That's kind of different from how we treat betrayers, isn't it? We are angry, refuse to talk, gossip up a storm about that person, and ice him or her with a vengeance. Not so, with Jesus.

> *But when the morning had now come, Jesus stood on the shore. . . . And He said to them, "Cast the net on the right side of the boat, and you will find some (fish)." So they cast, and now they were not able to draw it in because of the multitude of fish. Then, as soon as they had come to land, they saw a fire of coals there, and fish laid on it, and bread. . . . Jesus said to them, "Come and eat breakfast."* **—John 21:4–6, 9–12**

What a great story! Jesus came and found Peter. This is the God we love and serve, the One who desires so intensely to be with us that He comes to us even when we have sinned.

Jesus wanted to be restored to Peter just as He longs to be restored to you! When most people receive offenders, they wait with an angry face for an apology. But Jesus came where they were:

✦ To demonstrate His power by providing a huge catch of fish;

✦ To show His personal love with a cooked breakfast.

Could Jesus forgive this one who had been entrusted with walking with Him through His earthly ministry yet betrayed Him at His time of deepest need? Could He ever use a person whose life was marred by anger, cursing, lying, and denial?

It's hard to imagine when it happens. It's difficult to understand how deep the grace of God is, how rich is His mercy. But He does forgive, and He does restore.

What needs to happen in your heart so that you can share this good news with others?

Who do you know that needs the good news of restoration and forgiveness?

Pray for that opportunity to share with him or her this week.

WORSHIP IN THE STORM

God uses our mistakes to purify our hearts and to make us stronger for His service. He takes our adversity of choice and writes a story for others to learn from, for future generations to remember.

Jesus personally restored Peter, and Scripture records both sides of his story: the failure, and, later, the success. These were recorded for our benefit that we might not allow failure or discouragement to rule, but to walk in the light of His love.

The adversity of choice is healed when we repent of our sin and accept the intimate care of Christ for our lives to begin again. It happened for Peter; it can happen for you.

Peter wrote to warn all of us: "Be sober, be vigilant; because your adversary the devil *walks about like a roaring lion, seeking whom he may devour*" (1 Peter 5:8; emphasis added). No doubt he was remembering his own mistakes when he wrote these words.

God used the adversity of choice in Peter's life to completely transform and embolden him in a way that he might have never known before. Peter was so impacted by the Lord's deep mercy and so intensely grateful for Christ that he ended up a martyr for His name, persecuted and then crucified.[4] When he was put to death for the sake of Christ, Peter's proclamation was positive for Christ as well as public. In fact, many historians believe and tradition holds that Peter chose to be crucified upside down because he did not feel worthy to die in the same manner as his Lord.[5]

Adversity of choice changed Peter's life and the lives of countless thousands for generations. And it can change yours!

FUSE BOX

It is through trial and adversity that God
purifies and shapes our hearts so that
we can reflect His grace to others.

PRIVATE WORLD DEVOTIONS

MONDAY: See it. Read the surrounding passages or chapter for the Key Scripture so that you can get an understanding of the background and context. This helps you to really *see* the verse.

TUESDAY: Hear it. Read the daily Key Scripture and/or surrounding passage out loud, putting your name in, if applicable. For example, <u>John</u> *can do all things through Christ. Thieves have come to destroy* <u>John</u>*, but Jesus has come that* <u>John</u> *might have eternal life.*

WEDNESDAY: Write it. Write the verse and then what it says about:

✦ *Others:* Respond, serve, and love as Jesus would.

✦ *Me:* Specific attitudes, choices, or habits.

✦ *God:* His love, mercy, holiness, peace, joy, etc.

PRIVATE WORLD JOURNAL

I am grateful for—I praise You for—I am feeling—I am thinking—I need help with

PRIVATE WORLD DEVOTIONS *(Continued)*

THURSDAY: Memorize it. Take the verse with you—write it on a card or put it in your phone, iPod, or PDA. Go over it throughout the day so that it begins to *live* in your heart and mind.

FRIDAY: Pray it. Personalize the verse as you pray for yourself or for others or in praise to God. To pray is literally "to think about." Try thinking out loud or writing in your **PRIVATE WORLD JOURNAL**.

SATURDAY: Share it. Ask the Lord to bring someone to mind or in your path today who needs good news. Don't be shy—just let it out! Whether you IM, write, text, tell, or send it, the joy of God's Word will flow from your heart into theirs.

PRAYER REQUESTS

Date	Name	Need	Answer

PRIVATE WORLD JOURNAL

I am grateful for—I praise You for—I am feeling—I am thinking—I need help with

NOTES

CHAPTER 8

WORSHIP IN THE STORM

IS GOD IN CONTROL?

KEY SCRIPTURE

All the earth shall worship You and sing praises to You; they shall sing praises to Your name.

—Psalm 66:4

IT COULD BE YOU!

Take a look at these headlines taken from the *USA Today* Web site, all of which were posted in the same twenty-four-hour time period:

OPPORTUNITY:

"New Backpack Puts the Juice in Power Walking"

WASHINGTON—As soldiers, hikers and students can testify, it takes energy to haul around a heavy backpack. Now, researchers have developed a backpack that turns that energy into electricity.[1]

STORMS:

"Ophelia Strengthens to a Hurricane Again: Tropical Storm Ophelia Strengthens Into Hurricane Again and Could Hit the Atlantic Coast"

FLAGLER BEACH, Fla. (AP)—Tropical Storm Ophelia strengthened into a hurricane again Saturday as it charted a course that could lead it to the Atlantic coast.[2]

> Unmet needs and hurt emotions turn into greater personal pain.

SURVIVAL:

"Charities Call for More Katrina Donations Despite Fed Aid"

NEW YORK (AP)—Even with Congress earmarking billions of federal dollars for Hurricane Katrina relief, private charities are urging donors to keep on giving, contending their field operations remain crucial in meeting emergency needs and ensuring long-term aid to the worst-off victims.[3]

RECOVERY:

"Four Years After 9/11, New York Is Back"

NEW YORK—Four years after the Sept. 11 terror attacks crippled the city's travel and tourism industry, visitors once again love New York.[4]

WHY KNOW IT?

✦ At any given moment, there are an estimated 2,000 thunderstorms in progress over Earth's surface. These storms can vary from relatively mild rainstorms to very damaging storms that feature hail and high wind.[5]

✦ There are 439,000 references to "unprecedented opportunity" on the Web.[6]

✦ Members of the United Nations Disaster Assessment and Coordination team are permanently on stand-by to deploy to relief missions following disasters and humanitarian emergencies anywhere in the world.[7]

transfuse (trans FYOOZ) : to cause to pass from one to another; transmit

If you think that a day in the life of global news media bears a striking resemblance to a day in the life of a student, you are right! On any given day, you might:

+ face a *storm* or *disaster*;

+ cope with *survival*;

+ work to *recover* from problems;

+ be presented with exciting new *opportunities*.

Even in your own town, a disaster relief or rescue may be underway on one side, while across town, businesses are meeting to discuss new technology and markets for expansion. In your church, a missions committee might be meeting to discuss ministering to the impoverished while another committee down the hall is discussing how to build more space to deal with growth and opportunity.

That's life, or what is commonly referred to as the real world. It comes in what the Bible calls seasons, a period of time for either opportunity or difficulty.

Then those men, when they had seen the sign that Jesus did, said, "This is truly the Prophet who is to come into the world." Therefore when Jesus perceived that they were about to come and take Him by force to make Him king, He departed again to the mountain by Himself alone. —**John 6:14–15**

Sometimes, everything in life just clicks. Friends are good, the family is getting along, and all seems right in the world. The Greeks described *opportunity* as "a favorable wind." It's those days when the sails are full and the wind is blowing just right.

That's what the disciples were finally experiencing. First called by faith to leave behind family and security, they followed Christ. After a while, miracles began to happen more regularly, and they were astounded at the developing popularity of the Savior. Once unsure of their calling, now they rejoiced to be a part of this ministry.

infuse (in FYOOZ)**:** to cause to be permeated with something (as a principle or quality) that alters usually for the better

Winds of Opportunity

Thousands gathered on the hillside to hear and see Jesus. There wasn't a Chick-fil-A around the corner, so the question came up, "How will these people eat?" No one wanted Jesus to stop teaching and healing, but the disciples had to face reality: it was lunchtime, and the people were getting hungry.

> Oh come,
> let us sing to the Lord! Let us shout joyfully to the Rock of our salvation. Let us come before His presence with thanksgiving; Let us shout joyfully to Him with psalms. For the Lord is the great God, And the great King above all gods.
> —Psalm 95:1–3

Jesus wasn't worried about the situation. "What do you have?" He asked the disciples and then proceeded to multiply one boy's five loaves of bread and two fishes into food for thousands. The crowd went wild. So amazing was the outcome of Jesus' public works that the people wanted to "take Him by force to make Him king" (John 6:15). Jesus, knowing this was not the time for popularity contests and public shows, went up into the mountains alone to wait on God's perfect timing for His life and ministry.

He also sent His disciples away. The Scripture says, "Jesus *made* His disciples get into the boat and go before Him to the other side, while He sent the multitudes away" (Matthew 14:22; emphasis added).

The wind was blowing just right.

You can imagine this scene—exhilarated, tired, confident, and ready for the next big thing, the disciples obeyed and took the boat to the other side of the lake, away from the crowds, and away from Jesus.

✦ They were happy.

✦ They had been obedient.

✦ They were walking in the will of God.

No one expected anything but joy—until the storm came.

Then Came the Rain

The boat was now in the middle of the sea, tossed by the waves, for the wind was contrary. —**Matthew 14:24**

You have to understand the geography of the Sea of Galilee to understand just how quickly this storm probably came upon them. The Sea of Galilee lies 680 feet below sea level. It is bounded by hills, especially on the east side where they reach 2,000 feet high. These heights are a source of cool, dry air; but around the sea, the climate is semitropical with warm, moist air. The large difference in height between surrounding land and the sea causes large temperature and pressure changes, resulting in strong winds dropping to the sea . . . directly to the center of the lake with violent results . . . Small boats caught out on the sea are in immediate danger.[8]

Just how bad was this storm? Matthew was there, and in chapter 14 of his Gospel, he wrote that the boat was:

✦ "tossed by the waves," literally in the Greek, it was "tortured" (v. 24);[9]

✦ "the wind was contrary," describing it as a hostile enemy (v. 24);[10]

◆ "the wind was boisterous," a Greek word used to describe something strong and violent (v. 30).[11]

Strong language, right? No one wants to admit to feeling so hopeless. But in order to win over adversity, we have to be willing to face the pain. Do not deny, spiritualize, or minimize the pain that you experience, whether it involves rejection, neglect, ridicule, criticism, manipulation, or abandonment.

Do any of these terms describe how you feel now or how you have felt in the past about circumstances beyond your control?

◆ *tortured*

◆ *hostile enemy*

◆ *strong and violent*

Think about a time when you felt emotionally out of control, and circumstances were like a storm around you (friendship or family conflict, wrong choice, illness, etc.).

When was it?

Who was involved?

How did you feel?

_____

_____

_____

How did the storm end?

_____

_____

_____

> Faith is the opposite of *doubt*.
>
> Steadfast is the opposite of *waver*.

What do you wish you had done differently?

_____

_____

_____

This was no ordinary rain shower. What do you think the conversation in that boat was like? One minute, the disciples were giving high-fives all around, talking of an amazing future, and then, *boom!* They cry out, "We're going die right here!"

STORM SURVIVAL SKILLS

The Blame Game

The most popular coping method of this generation is *the blame game*. If there's danger, if there's fear, if we're going to be angry . . . don't we need to find someone to blame this on and be mad at?

You can imagine that the conversation on the boat went something like this that day on the lake: "Whose *fault* is it that we are in this storm?"

And each had their theory:

+ Peter chose the wrong spot in the lake.

+ John didn't bring the right boat.

+ Matthew shouldn't have tried to collect that last tax.

+ Andrew didn't bring the poor man up the mountain.

+ It must be Satan's fault.

In this story, all of the above statements were false. If you want to blame someone in this situation, blame the will of God. Remember, Matthew said that Jesus "made" them go into the boat.

What? Seriously, take a look at the verse again:

> *Immediately Jesus made His disciples*
> *get into the boat and go before Him to*
> *the other side.* —**Matthew 14:22**

The disciples were in:

+ God's timing ("immediately")

+ God's will (Jesus "made" them go)

+ God's direction (Jesus told them to "go . . . to the other side")

Jesus did not *cause* the storm. But Jesus did *allow* the disciples to be *in the storm*.

When you're in the storm, playing the blame game will not protect you from the rain, and it will not get you out of the wind.

ASK YOURSELF

How does the hurt work as an obstacle to moving forward in life? Does it bring depression, discouragement, or low self-image? Take a moment to think through how the pain of adversity is affecting you.

The Fear Factor

> *Now in the fourth watch of the night Jesus went to them, walking on the sea. And when the disciples saw Him walking on the sea, they were troubled, saying, "It is a ghost!" And they cried out for fear. But immediately Jesus spoke to them, saying, "Be of good cheer! It is I; do not be afraid."* —**Matthew 14:25–27**

The disciples were spending the night in the boat; most likely, it was their "hotel" for the night. The night would have been divided into four watches, the periods into which the time between sunset and sunrise was divided. They are so called because watchmen relieved each other at each of these periods.[12] The fourth watch was between 3:00 a.m and 6:00 a.m. It was still very dark, which explains why the figure of Jesus could have looked like a ghost.

We know from studying this passage that Jesus was up on the mountain, and He had a clear view of the disciples below in the boat. Why, then, did He wait until the fourth watch to come and help them?

Sometimes God allows us time to process our emotions so that we can choose whether we will retreat in fear or boldly find a way through.

We retreat when we:

✦ blame anyone we can;

✦ complain to anyone who will listen;

✦ fearfully imagine the worst.

The disciples had time to do this while Jesus watched nearby. Possibly, He needed these disciples to learn that *survival in any storm is not about who to blame; it's about who to trust.*

The top four positive emotions that I want to develop in the next six weeks are:

1._____   2. _____

3._____   4. _____

To do this, I need to process the pain of the past.

I am still affected by the storm that happened in my life _____ (days, weeks, months, years) ago. Recognizing this, I can now begin to work through the storm conditions and into peace.

diffuse (di FYOOZ); to pour out and permit or cause to spread freely; to extend, scatter

A Bold Move of Faith

> *And Peter answered Him and said, "Lord, if it is You, command me to come to You on the water." So He said, "Come." And when Peter had come down out of the boat, he walked on the water to go to Jesus.* —**Matthew 14:28–29**

Peter surveyed the situation—storm all around, a ship held hostage by violent waves. He would probably be tossed into the sea at any moment. Should he wait for the storm to overturn the boat or choose to go to Jesus and risk drowning anyway?

Peter surveyed the situation and realized the inevitable: *if you want to get out of a boat that is in danger, then you have to stand up and walk forward.*

 In any adversity, there are always three choices:

1. Be angry, stall, and try to cope.

2. Wait to see what everyone else will do.

3. Boldly trust in Christ and move forward.

The Christian leader chooses #3, even though it may take some time to get there.

ASK YOURSELF

Which choice are you working through right now?

Why do you think that is?

Which one do you want to choose?

What is ONE THING you can do to move forward in your personal faith? Choose one:

- ✦ Surrender to God's will as you move forward.

- ✦ Admit the pain you are feeling and talk to a friend or family member about it.

- ✦ Decide to put the past behind and no longer allow it to rule your thought life.

- ✦ Believe God wants the best for you.

How will you do that ONE THING this week?

He'll Meet You There

> *But when he saw that the wind was boisterous, he was afraid; and beginning to sink he cried out, saying, "Lord, save me!" And immediately Jesus stretched out His hand and caught him, and said to him, "O you of little faith, why did you doubt?"* **—Matthew 14:30–31**

The moment that Peter took his eyes off Jesus, he saw that the wind was boisterous, and the circumstances became more potent than his faith. In the midst of the rescue, Peter doubted.

Jesus understood Peter's heart and immediately stretched out His hand to rescue him. Wow! Wouldn't you have loved to see that?

Praise God for a Savior who is willing to get wet with you, a Savior who meets you in the middle of the storm.

 What are some things about Christ that you might be changing your mind about?

+ His love ("If He loves me, why am I going through this?")

+ His power ("If He is all-powerful, why does the world feel out of control?")

+ His will ("This seems too hard for me. I need to empty out the negative.")

Write it:

_____

_____

_____

Peter may have wavered, but Jesus didn't change His mind because of it. He rescued Peter and waited patiently for him to have the faith to "come" to Him.

Our recovery from the storm does not depend on:

+ outward circumstances, or

+ our ability to hold on.

Recovery Results in Worship

> *And when they got into the boat, the wind ceased. Then those who were in the boat came and worshiped Him, saying, "Truly You are the Son of God." —**Matthew 14:32–33***

Two wonderful things happened here!

✦ Peter learned firsthand that faith is about taking that first step into the unknown.

✦ Those with him learned that Jesus is who He says He is and does what He says He will do.

We see that the disciples made a conscious decision that day to *worship,* as a result of the storm's events. From this day on, they would:

✦ surrender spiritually, emotionally, and mentally to Christ;

✦ believe in His purpose and power for their lives;

✦ trust in His timing for each day;

✦ take Him at His Word.

Never waste your sorrows, but always share the joy of worship you find in trusting God. Think about it: If you meet someone who is going through some of the difficulty you have faced, what will you say? Choose two Scriptures to memorize, and have them ready:

1.

2.

WORSHIP IN THE STORM

In the midst of every storm, we must be willing to believe that:

✦ *God is more than able to stop the storm.* "The Lord has His way in the whirlwind and in the storm, and the clouds are the dust of His feet" (Nahum 1:3).

✦ *God has authority over every storm.* "He alone spreads out the heavens, and treads on the waves of the sea" (Job 9:8).

✦ *God will come to us in the storm.* "In the fourth watch of the night Jesus went to them, walking on the sea" (Matthew 14:25).

[FUSE BOX]

To worship Christ is to believe *He is worthy* of our trust, respect, time, and choices.

Doubt = Change of mind or heart

PRIVATE WORLD DEVOTIONS

MONDAY: See it. Read the surrounding passages or chapter for the Key Scripture so that you can get an understanding of the background and context. This helps you to really *see* the verse.

TUESDAY: Hear it. Read the daily Key Scripture and/or surrounding passage out loud, putting your name in, if applicable. For example, <u>John</u> *can do all things through Christ. Thieves have come to destroy* <u>John</u>, *but Jesus has come that* <u>John</u> *might have eternal life.*

WEDNESDAY: Write it. Write the verse and then what it says about:

+ *Others:* Respond, serve, and love as Jesus would.
+ *Me:* Specific attitudes, choices, or habits.
+ *God:* His love, mercy, holiness, peace, joy, etc.

PRIVATE WORLD JOURNAL

I am grateful for—I praise You for—I am feeling—I am thinking—I need help with

PRIVATE WORLD DEVOTIONS *(Continued)*

THURSDAY: Memorize it. Take the verse with you—write it on a card or put it in your phone, iPod, or PDA. Go over it throughout the day so that it begins to *live* in your heart and mind.

FRIDAY: Pray it. Personalize the verse as you pray for yourself or for others or in praise to God. To pray is literally "to think about." Try thinking out loud or writing in your **PRIVATE WORLD JOURNAL.**

SATURDAY: Share it. Ask the Lord to bring someone to mind or in your path today who needs good news. Don't be shy—just let it out! Whether you IM, write, text, tell, or send it, the joy of God's Word will flow from your heart into theirs.

PRAYER REQUESTS

Date	Name	Need	Answer

PRIVATE WORLD JOURNAL

I am grateful for—I praise You for—I am feeling—I am thinking—I need help with

Notes

CHAPTER 1—STUFF HAPPENS: WHY DO BAD THINGS HAPPEN TO GOOD PEOPLE?

1. *Merriam-Webster Online Dictionary* (2005), s.v. "adversity," http://www.m-w.com/dictionary.htm.

2. *The American Heritage Dictionary of the English Language,* 4th ed. (Amerian Heritage, 2000), s.v. "adversity."

3. Hank Hanegraaff, *The Bible Answer Book* (Nashville: J Countryman, 2004), 170–71.

4. John Phillips, *Exploring Hebrews* (Chicago: Moody, 1977), 192.

CHAPTER 2—STUFF HAPPENS: WHY DOES IT HAVE TO HAPPEN TO ME?

1. Kidzworld, "Get the 411 on Teen Depression," http://www.kidzworld.com/site/p4446.htm. Copyright ©2005 Kidzworld Media. All rights reserved.

2. The Barna Group, Ltd, "People's Faith Flavor Influences How They See Themselves," http://www.barna.org/FlexPage.aspx?Page = BarnaUpdate&BarnaUpdateID = 119 (accessed December 20, 2005).

3. Diane Raso Strack, "New Start for Single Moms", Chapter 8, "Transforming Thinking Patterns," (First Orlando Publishing, Orlando, 2004).

CHAPTER 3—I KNOW THE VERSES: WHY AM I SO AFRAID?

1. Global Security, "The World at War: Current Conflicts," http://www.globalsecurity.org/military/world/war/ (accessed August 7, 2005).

1. Daniel Yee, "Report: Teens Fear School Violence," http://www.cbsnews.com/stories/2004/07/29/national/main632972.shtml (accessed December 20, 2005).

CHAPTER 4—LEAVE ME ALONE!: BUT DOES ANYBODY CARE?

1. Joel Engle, testimony. www.joelengle.com. Used by permission.

2. Barry Kliff, "Heading Toward a Fatherless Society," MSNBC, www.msnbc.com, March 31, 1999.

CHAPTER 5—THIS STUFF IS TOO HARD: WHY AM I SO STRESSED?

1. About, Inc., "Teen Stress," http://panicdisorder.about.com/cs/youthanxiety/a/teenstress.htm (accessed December 20, 2005).

2. John Fetto, "First Comes Love—Teen Dating Statistics," American Demographics, June 1, 2003.

3. *Wikipedia*, s.v. "Selah", http://en.wikipedia.org/wiki/Selah (accessed December 20, 2005).

4. Franklin Covey, Effectiveness Zone: What Matters Most Learning Center, "Mastering Information Overload," http://www.franklincovey.com.

CHAPTER 6—THE ADVERSITY OF NO CHOICE: WHAT DOES GOD WANT FROM ME?

1. Council of Chief State School Officers, "States and CCSSO Respond to the Hurricanes," http://www.ccsso.org/whats_new/6907.cfm (accessed December 21, 2005).

2. PBS, "Children and Armed Conflict," http://www.pbs.org/newshour/bb/international/jan-june05/un_3-10.html (accessed December 21, 2005).

3. Joseph Thayer and George Abbot-Smith, *The KJV New Testament Greek Lexicon*, s.v. "pascho," http://www.biblestudytools.net Lexicons/Greek/grk.cgi?number = 3958&version = kjv.

4. John Wesley, *Explanatory Notes on the Whole Bible* (1765), s. v. "Mark 14." http://bible.crosswalk.com/Commentaries/Wesleys ExplanatoryNotes/wes.cgi?book = mr&chapter = 014.

5. John Gill, *Exposition on the Old and New Testaments* (Grand Rapids: Baker, 1982), s.v. "Mark 14:33," http://bible.crosswalk.com/Commentaries/GillsExpositionoftheBible/gil.cgi?book = mr&chapter = 014&verse = 033&next = 034&prev = 032.

CHAPTER 7—THE ADVERSITY OF BAD CHOICES: WHY DID I DO THAT?

1. About, Inc., "Teen Pregnancy Statistics," http://womensissues. about.com/od/statistics/a/teenpregstats.htm (accessed December 21, 2005).

2. Focus Adolescent Services, "Drugs and Teen Substance Abuse," http://www.focusas.com/SubstanceAbuse.html (accessed December 21, 2005).

3. William Barclay, *The Gospel of Mark,* rev. ed. (Philadelphia: The Westminster Press, 1975), 342.

4. Eusebius, *Church History: Book Two,* chapter 25. Available at http://www.newadvent.org/fathers/2501.htm.

5. *Wikipedia,* s.v. "Saint Peter," http://en.wikipedia.org/wiki/Saint_ Peter.

CHAPTER 8—WORSHIP IN THE STORM: IS GOD IN CONTROL?

1. Randolph E. Schmid, "New backpack puts the juice in power walking," *USA Today,* September 8, 2005, http://www.usatoday. com/tech/products/gear/2005-09-08-electric-backpack_x.htm.

2. Travis Reed, "Ophelia Strengthens to a Hurricane Again: Tropical Storm Ophelia Strengthens Into Hurricane Again and Could Hit the Atlantic Coast," *USA Today,* September 10, 2005, http://abcnews. go.com/US/wireStory?id = 1113789&CMP = OTC-RSSFeeds0312.

3. "Charities call for more Katrina donations despite fed aid," *USA Today,* September 9, 2005, http://www.usatoday.com/news/ nation/2005-09-09-katrinacharities_x.htm.

4. Barbara De Lollis and Laura Petrecca, "Four Years After 9/11, New York Is Back," USA Today, September 8, 2005, http://usatoday. printthis.clickability.com/pt/cpt?action = cpt&title = USATODAY. com + - + Four + years + after + 9 % 2F11 % 2C + New + York + is + back&expire = &urlID = 15474365&fb = Y&url = http % 3A % 2F % 2 Fwww.usatoday.com % 2Fmoney % 2F2005-09-08-new-york-usat_ x.htm&partnerID = 1661.

5. Annenburg/CPS Learner.org, "Eye of the Storm: Inside a Hurricane," http://www.learner.org/exhibits/weather/storms2.html (accessed December 21, 2005).

6. Google.com, search for "unprecedented opportunity," http://www. google.com/search?hl = en&lr = &rls = GGLD%2CGGLD%3A2004-31%2CGGLD%3Aen&q = %22unprecedented + opportunity%22& btnG = Search (accessed September 10, 2005).

7. UNDAC, "Humanitarian Issues," http://ochaonline.un.org/webpage. asp?Nav = _humanissues_en&Site = _humanissues.

8. Dr. Donald B. DeYoung, *Weather & the Bible* "What's Special About the Sea of Galilee?"(Grand Rapids: Baker, 1992), as quoted at http://christiananswers.net/q-eden/ednk-seaofgalilee.html.

9. Joseph Thayer and George Abbot-Smith, *The KJV New Testament Greek Lexicon,* s.v. "basanizo," http://www.biblestudytools.net/ Lexicons/Greek/grk.cgi?number = 928&version = kjv (accessed December 21, 2005).

10. Joseph Thayer and George Abbot-Smith, *The KJV New Testament Greek Lexicon,* s.v. "enantios," http://www.biblestudytools.net/ Lexicons/Greek/grk.cgi?number = 1727&version = kjv (accessed December 21, 2005).

11. Joseph Thayer and George Abbot-Smith, *The KJV New Testament Greek Lexicon,* s.v. "ischuros," http://www.biblestudytools.net/ Lexicons/Greek/grk.cgi?number = 2478&version = kjv (accessed December 21, 2005).

12. Christians Answers.net, s.v. "watches," http://christiananswers. net/dictionary/watches.html (accessed December 21, 2005).

ABOUT THE AUTHORS

Jay Strack, president and founder of Student Leadership University, is an inspiring and effective communicator, author, and minister. Acclaimed by leaders in the business world, religious affiliations, and education realms as a dynamic speaker, Jay has spoken to an estimated 15 million people in his 30 years of ministry. His versatile style has been presented across the country and in 22 countries, before government officials, corporate groups, numerous professional sports teams in the NFL, NBA, and MLB, to over 9,500 school assemblies, and at some 100 universities. Zig Ziglar calls Jay Strack, "entertaining, but powerful, inspiring and informative."

Diane Raso Strack is the co-founder of Student Leadership University and a Franklin-Covey life-management facilitator. She is the author and founder of *New Start 4 Single Moms* and co-author of *Good Kids Who Do Bad Things*.

Lead, follow or be bait.

This is where the journey begins – SLU101!

At Student Leadership University, you won't find canoes and campfires. What you will find is a 4-day comprehensive program designed to catapult you into a life of confidence, significance, and leadership. SLU prepares you to successfully navigate the shark-infested waters of our culture with the rules and tools of leadership. Stop hanging out with the bait fish. Come to SLU where dreaming is encouraged and the language of leadership is spoken freely.

Explore the possibilities at
www.studentleadership.net

Student
Leadership
UNIVERSITY

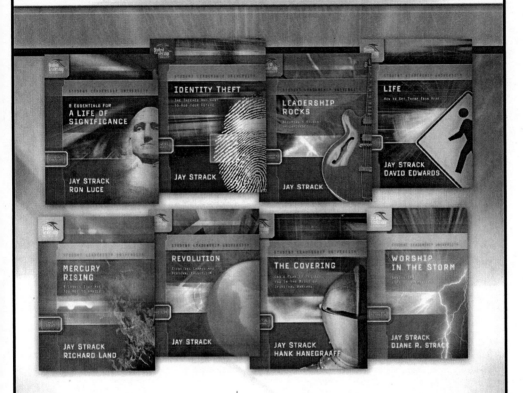

CPSIA information can be obtained at www.ICGtesting.com
Printed in the USA
LVOW11s2325221114

414938LV00018B/51/P